Pronto!

Writings from Rome

Pronto!

Writings from Rome

edited by
John Tullius

WRITERS
HOUSE
BOOKS

A Writers House Book
TripleTree Publishing
PO Box 5684, Eugene, OR 97405
(541) 338-3184 – www.TripleTreePub.com

Cover and interior design by Alan M. Clark
Cover photos by Al Cratty
Printed in the United States of America
1 2 3 4 5 6 7 8 9

All royalties from the sale of this book
will be donated to the
Maui Writers Foundation
Young Writers Scholarship Program

Table of Contents

Introduction

Rome is a city of layers. Civilizations buried. Cities under cities. Catacombs.

Rome is an archeologist's dream.

But what the archeologists find of significance is art. Art created with great passion. Art in Rome is revealed layer by layer. Unlike geologic layers of sediment, or a deluge of ash from Vesuvius, the art was created one piece at a time, one artist at a time, one vision at a time. Over four thousand years, it accumulates into impressive strata.

And so we came to Rome to write. To experience the artists who had come before us and be inspired by them.

Thirty-four writers, five professional instructors and a rigorous writing curriculum in a city like no other. Many distractions, not the least of which is *Roma* herself.

The goal was to have the attendees write as they had never written before: fast, hard, urgent. Armed with notebook and camera, each attendee arrived fresh, with no writing to rework, and no preconceived ideas to live up to. Completely different from the Maui Writers Retreat, where attendees bring work they wish to improve, in Rome they were to create three different pieces on the spot. Each group had two days with a set of professional team leaders, then it moved on to different instructors, a different theory of authorship, a different area of Rome to explore.

John Saul and Mike Sack paired their attendees and sent them on a hunt to find a "what if" story line. This is their famed technique: to define a story line in 25 words or less.

Dorothy Allison and I teamed up to encourage the writers to observe both character traits and sensory images, admonishing them to pay attention to the tiny things that captured not only their attention, but their passion.

Terry Brooks worked on "dreaming the story." His technique is to use reality as a springboard. Take what you see and reflect on the story it suggests.

To make the deadlines more difficult, we besieged the group with stunning field trips: Pompeii, dinner with the Tenors, lunch at the Temple of the Vestal Virgins, the Sistine Chapel, the gardens at Tivoli, the claustrophobic catacombs, the Colosseum, the Pantheon, St. Peter's Basilica, watching the cameo carvers at work. And more. Much more. Much more pasta, *vino*, laughter, pasta, *vino*, tears, pasta, *vino*, shopping, pasta, *vino*, *gelato*. We didn't intentionally reduce the writing time available; we intentionally reduced the sleeping time available.

The attendees learned a few things about themselves in this process. They learned that inspiration comes from focusing on the tiny things. They learned that there are many ways to approach the craft. They learned that they could write on demand, and write well. They discovered that practice greases the process. They learned the value of setting aside a first draft and returning to polish it later. They learned that there is no wrong way, and no right way, merely their way, and it is unique in the universe, just like each personality. And they discovered that one must write many words before a story emerges on the emulsion of their experience.

Attendees came from four countries and thirteen states, but left as a unified group of Roman writers. Friendships became welded so tightly that no number of miles or years will crack the bonds. John & Shannon

Tullius, with the help of Roberto Miglio, created an extraordinary opportunity to write and to learn.

We had an exceptional time and produced some exceptional work—stories, essays and poems so good we couldn't keep them to ourselves.

Here, then, are thirty-eight pieces of Rome. A peephole, if you will, into the continuing tradition of contributing art to Rome.

—Elizabeth Engstrom
June, 2002

Poetic

by John Tullius

I saw her only twice, well, three times if you count her pictures below the headlines in the Italian dailies declaring she was murdered.

I was standing outside the Keats and Shelley Museum in *Piazza di Spagna*, busily tending to a gelato the first time I saw her. It was a favorite spot of my wife Helen's. We'd usually have an espresso sitting on the Spanish Steps while I read the *Herald Trib* and she hummed her way through a book of Romantics. She'd look up after some stanza and sip her coffee with a look of glazed approval that always made me smile. Keats, Shelley, Byron were pabulum for my taste. A hearty dose of Greene acid was what it took to sear to the heart of the matter for me. That was Helen and I, two beings hurtling in from opposite ends of the emotional universe.

The truth was we just fell—swiftly, urgently, without philosophy or poetry, for one another. I thought she was beautiful, of course, but there was a fragrance to her, a slightly high-pitched erotic taste more powerful in the end than all the sonnets strung together, that drew my lips to hers. What mesmerized me though was the way she held herself, the way she stood, her unmistakable walk. It was a grace that rose directly from her soul and saturated her every muscle and bone.

A friend once tried to compliment her by saying,

"God, your wife walks just like a runway model, or something."

Or something.

"That's the dumbest damn thing I've ever heard," I shot back at him. I would have sooner forgiven him if he'd announced they'd been seeing each other. I lost my taste for him after that, like a novelist who's a decent storyteller but whose prose is so ham-fisted one day you just can't stomach his graceless existence anymore. And give him up.

It was Gabriela in motion that caught in my vision that morning, as she came out of *Trinita dei Monti*. After she descended the steps of the church, she disappeared among the vendor's umbrellas and the artist's easels below. Just long enough for me to question what I'd seen. Was it just me still catching glimpses of Helen everywhere I went? Then, suddenly, there she was at the top of the Spanish Steps, making her way down the long processional, her shoulders level as water, her chin elevated as if a lover's fingertips had raised it for a kiss. I'd only seen that bearing, yes that was it, that bearing, in one other person.

The poetry evaporated from my life when Helen died. It had been more than a year and I still had the dead feeling in my stomach that had gripped me at her funeral. My friends had wanted me to get away, to get some distance from all those memories of Helen, so they pitched in for a golf vacation to Scotland. But when I got to Heathrow, I passed Alitalia and like an addict, my compulsion drove me to take the next plane to Rome, Helen's favorite place on earth, the place where we made love every morning even when we were bickering. And afterwards, we'd always seem to end up at *Piazza di Spagna* to start the day.

By now I was just staring at Gabriela, the gelato running down my hand. The azaleas were in bloom, a riot of magenta cascading down the sides of the Steps. Gabriela seemed undistracted by the commotion of color and the labyrinth of people filling the steps. She wove her way deftly through the clusters of kids and tourists sitting on the steps talking, stretched out for the sun, a guitar or two being strummed, lips being kissed.

When she drew close, a gaggle of boys jumped up in front of her, grabbing their backpacks and guitars, shaking hands three different ways, hugging and backslapping. It forced her to stop a few feet from where I stood. That's when I noticed her make-up, too heavy around her cheek and neck. Helen had applied it thick that way when she was sunburned. Gabriela had on a silk scarf that covered a lot of her face, but it didn't hide a deep bruise on her neck up near her ear, the shape of a thumb. To the side of her dark sunglasses I could see an ugly purple, the color of a bruised peach, throbbing below her eyes.

Suddenly the boys parted and she was gone across the piazza and down *via Condotti*. I trotted a few feet to the fountain and watched as she made her way down the narrow street, watched the beauty of her movement and saw what I couldn't see as she descended the steps— she was limping slightly. It was the most heartbreaking thing I'd witnessed since they'd lowered Helen's coffin into that hole.

I saw her again a couple of days later. I'd dropped a friend at the airport, saw him to his gate, kissed both his cheeks, and watched him disappear through the departure gate. She passed me as I was lowering my wave.

It was her walk that turned my head, of course, because I couldn't have recognized her. No one could have. She had on an ill-fitting skirt and a bunchy sweater and she was wearing a grey wig, tied tight with a worn woolen scarf. She was dressed like the old women behind the stalls in *Campo di Fiore*. She had on the shoes of a seventy-year-old as well, thick heels and rounded toes. And she still hid behind the dark glasses and the heavy make-up.

I turned and followed her as she walked to a nearby

gate. It was an effective disguise. Except from me. I knew that walk in my dreams.

She sat down and dropped her chin to her breast, covering herself with a shawl. I stood in the news shop across the way for twenty minutes thumbing through magazines, watching her. When her flight was finally called, she walked through the departure gate alone. I wanted to get on that flight with her to Geneva. But I didn't. She was going on a journey as lonely as my own. And it was going to be a long time before either of our hearts would open wide enough for another being to enter.

Two mornings later the Italian papers were full of her. "Soccer Star's Wife Missing." She had disappeared four days before without a trace. I wondered where she'd stayed the first two nights while she hid from her husband, Francesco Milano, "the next Maradona," *Roma's* top scorer, a hero who'd almost single-handedly beaten the despised Brits in the Euro Cup.

Over the next week, another story came into focus one detail at a time. Neighbors reported on the beatings they'd heard Gabriela take, on the bruises and black eyes, and the broken bones. The *carabanieri* had been called a few times as well, but of course that had only turned into an autograph session with their hero, "Feet of Gold," as the sporting press had dubbed him. It didn't matter that he liked to kick his wife around too. Wait until they got back to the station and told their friends who they'd shaken hands with.

It probably killed them to have to bring him in, to force him to answer the questions that the press was insisting the whole of Italy was asking. Where was Gabriela? Or more to the point, where was her body? And where was Francesco the night his wife disappeared? Had they gotten into another alcohol-induced row (it had already come out that Milano had a bad drinking problem) and perhaps this time he'd gone too far? It went on for weeks, the suspicion hanging over him and deepening with every passing day, and every new piece of evidence the press dug up. The TV would show him arriving yet again at the *Polizia* with his lawyers—looking more beaten by the day, pale and haggard. And worst of all, he was playing poorly and his fans, the ones who had raised him to an arrogance so blinding that he thought it his right to batter such beauty, were losing patience.

I was at *Caffe Navona* sipping an espresso one morning when I came upon the delicious news in *Il Messaggero*. They'd arrested Golden Feet the previous night and it seemed certain that they were going to charge him with the murder of Gabriela Milano. There were just too many questions even for a soccer star—his broken knuckle (which he swore he'd injured in a game), Gabriela's blood on the wall of the bedroom (which his lawyer said could have been there for months), her frantic phone calls to friends begging for help (the fact that she'd told her sister that Francesco had said he'd kill her didn't help), and, of course, the official complaints she'd filed that the police had finally deemed *"importante."*

I finished my caffe and ordered another. It was spring in Rome and as the birds splashed around in Bernini's fountain across the way, I felt a sadness lifting from my chest. Beauty was all around me. Helen had taught me that.

I could, of course, have walked to the *Polizia* headquarters on *Via Vittorio Emmanuale* and cleared the whole thing up. But instead I thought I'd spend the morning walking around Rome, saying goodbye to the places that Helen and I had loved. Perhaps, I'd end up at Nino's for lunch. The wild boar and linguine with pesto and a bottle of red was her favorite. I was going to savor it the way I savored the secret I shared with Gabriela. It was the closest thing to the intimacy of love that I had felt for a very, very long time.

Little Jewels

by Robin Field Gainey

Shimoni negotiated the morning throng of pedestrians and darting Roman traffic with the distinctive aplomb of an urban dog. Employing the tangle of elaborate detail often defined by canine intellect, he careened a path in the direction of his apartment, keeping just far enough ahead of his Contessa to cause her irritation. A method he hoped would tempt her to a quickened pace for he was anxious to return home.

Allowed extra time off his leash, he took the opportunity to enjoy his freedom, lingering now and then over the marvelous filth of the Roman streets. He followed an array of tempting odors emerging from the many open doors along the way, indicating edibles of every kind, all urging his prompt attention. Accomplishing an invigorating dash across the hectic *via Corso*, he dodged a swarm of buzzing *motorini,* nearly catching a paw in the peril of a widened space between the cobblestones before plopping down in front of the entry to his building.

Shimoni knew his Contessa would chide his reckless behavior when she finally arrived, but the knowledge did nothing to slow him. The morning sun had piqued his thirst, and the daily turn around the park exhausted his reserves. He had spent his morning tearing and tumbling with the usual suspects on the flats above the Monte Pincio, covering all the marks he could find. Now his only thought was the food awaiting him in his kitchen. He was famished.

The end of the usual morning walk, so called *la passegiata* by his Contessa, the purchase of a *giornali*, and the taking of a *cappuccino* at the corner bar, all meant that food was the next order of business. Even though she had skipped the café stop this morning, returning them early, he was more than ready for his breakfast, eager for her to catch up and deliver him into the comfort of his apartment.

He watched his Contessa employ her customary caution as she crossed the street, and wondered if she had ever been brave enough to dare the chaotic traffic; if she had ever felt pleasant exhilaration at the buffeting wind that ran with the cars racing along the *Lungotevere* that skirted Rome's river. Had her ears ever been ruffled by the breeze of a Fiat passing close enough to provide a full lung of petrol fumes? He thought not, and was sorry, wondering what might return the sparkle to her eyes; eyes that used to flash like the lightning bugs he once glimpsed on a trip to the sea.

When his Contessa reached the door, she shot him a disapproving look. The tone of her voice revealed her irritation, yet she scooped him into her arms with a gentle touch and loving tousle of his head. She kissed him quickly; assurance that she continued to find him attractive and amusing despite his imprudent behavior. With a turn of a key the heavy outer doors opened and in one smooth motion down the hall they entered a tiny elevator. As they ascended, he used the time to lick the lipstick off his nose and swipe a paw over his head to smooth his hair. The rancid taste of the lipstick was not something he enjoyed, but it was a small price to pay for the ride.

He wagged his tail with great enthusiasm as the elevator set them free and they approached his apartment. When his Contessa opened the door he wiggled a leap from her arms and raced in the direction of the kitchen.

But his pace slowed when he caught sight of *il Conte*, the Count, standing at the sink carefully attending to something that the morning sun had set to sparkling in his hand. Usually absent upon their morning return, his presence disrupted the smooth reunion of Shimoni to his breakfast bowl, for he and the Count seldom enjoyed each other's company.

So he waited at the threshold to the kitchen, trying to determine the contents of the Count's hand, until his nose greeted the tiniest whiff of a ripened chestnut. It was the same sweet, musty odor of those he liked to eat that fell with the crisp leaves of autumn beneath the giant trees along the river, and he knew it must be a *marroni* pastry that the count held. His Contessa called them *gioielletti*, little jewels, and they were regarded as such by Shimoni. As precious as any fine gem, exquisite in taste and just as rare, for they were seldom available to a dog with acute concern for his figure.

With the slam of the heavy entry door behind his Contessa, the Count gave a startled jump, pushed a piece of paper into his pocket and the perfect small pastry lost its balance, falling from his nervous fingers in the direction of the floor. Without hesitation, Shimoni sprang to action, skating on long toenails across the ceramic floor to intercept the delight, anticipating the first crunch of the treat that would soon be his. A second later he sat at the feet of the Count, proud to have captured the piece in his mouth before it reached the floor.

The pastry, now a brief memory, had been swallowed whole. Though he loved to show off, in his haste he never truly appreciated those happy accidents as much as when they splattered on the hard tile and needed to be methodically licked away. The messier the floor, the more time the treat lingered on his tongue, cool whipping cream clinging to his whiskers, lengthening the pleasure of the incident and the memory that followed.

But this time the strike had been quick and clean, and the only real satisfaction lay in the knowledge that he had beaten the target to the tile. In fact, the jump had been quite high and both the landing and the swallow, painful. Feeling an uneasy lump in his throat, he looked up to see the Count glower at him in a most disquieting way.

Used to catching the Count giving him unhappy looks and unpleasant gestures, he knew the Count found him neither attractive nor amusing and he had to admit the feeling was mutual. Shimoni did not approve of the way the Count cared for his Contessa; did not like the coldness they shared. He did not understand why two people would keep themselves together if they revealed nothing that was gentle or affectionate. Shimoni certainly would run away if his Contessa cared for him in the same fashion she was cared for by the Count.

Affection seemed to be the tie that bound creatures together, he thought. Affection and treats. And he hadn't seen the two people give each other treats in a long, long time.

He swallowed hard and felt the painful lump begin to slide down his throat and as he did, the Count grabbed him in a very rude manner, turning him upside down and shaking him hard. Shimoni did not think of himself as a whiner, like some of the *molto elegante* dogs that frequented the *Pincio* in the mornings, but this action took him by surprise and a squeal escaped. The noise reminded him of a motor trip taken to his country house and the wild young pigs below the vineyard he had chased along the flats that bordered the creek. They squealed the same high pitch that was now coming from a place so deep inside himself he had not known it existed and he felt immediate regret for having frightened the piglets in such a way.

To his fortune the alarm prompted his Contessa to the rescue. She appeared in the company of a thunderous reproach aimed at the chagrined Count, and angry sounds echoed from the high vaulted ceiling. By the time Shimoni lay in the comfort and safety of her arms, he was shaking so violently that he thought he might be sick and, for a moment, he found fleeting pleasure in supposing he could lick the pastry from the cool tile after all. But as he and his Contessa settled into a puffy chair so did his stomach and all that remained was an uncomfortable lump sitting heavy in his belly.

The excitement had been so great that he had forgotten to eat his breakfast, but the thought of food was no longer attractive. Overcome by the fatigue often conveyed by sudden fright, he curled himself into a tight ball on his Contessa's lap. Drawing his paws under himself as far as he could, he tucked them carefully away, fearing the Count might pass by, pull him up and shake him by a flagrant leg. Shimoni slept away the day, and when his Contessa moved him onto the couch he hardly noticed.

As the winter sun began to fade into the late afternoon he was awakened by soft voices and raised his head to see the Count standing above him, holding his leash. He was startled by the rough manner in which the strap was attached to his collar and surprised that it was the Count, normally not interested in the company of dogs, who was leading him out the door and into the late day.

They took the stairway instead of the lift and Shimoni negotiated the four flights of slippery marble stairs carefully as the smooth stone could be a danger. Winding around the box elevator to the *terrazzo* below, Shimoni wondered if they would be meeting the woman who smelled of roses again. It was usually only on the colder evenings, when his Contessa did not care to walk too long in the bitter air, that the Count took him to the *Pincio* to visit the Rose Woman.

Shimoni did not mind the woman's company. She had a pleasant voice and often fed both of them treats she pulled from different bags. He had only ever seen her in the evenings, but had seen her regularly since the Count began last fall to accompany Shimoni on those last chance walks in the chilly twilight air.

His Contessa had not yet been introduced to the Rose

Woman but Shimoni felt very sure she might like her if they met. The two women were both very kind to him and it was clear to Shimoni, as it is to all dogs, that those who appreciate the company of canines share a singular bond. In fact, he began to enjoy the Rose Woman's company and the evening snacks in the park, finding the experience only dampened by the inescapable presence of the Count, for whom he could not understand any two people ever sharing a bond of any kind.

As soon as they were outside the building, the Count lit his pipe, pulled a plastic bag from his pocket and began to watch Shimoni with great interest. Indeed, in all his life, he felt this normally stolid man had never regarded him so carefully. Each time Shimoni hesitated the Count would take his pipe in hand, bend down through a ribbon of blue tobacco smoke and squint in the fading light to examine any business in which Shimoni was engaged.

It was a long walk, and in the cold season, not nearly as pleasant as the early evening *passegiata* he was used to taking with his Contessa in warmer weather. A balmier atmosphere allowed the fragrances of the day to linger long into the night, affording a small dog the pleasure of recalling the daily events that soared along the exhale of a frantic city in repose. The Count had not given him the comfort of a coat and as darkness fell over the dingy streets, Shimoni walked along in the dull, frosty air, pulling his tail down as tight as he could for warmth.

Even in the summer, he never enjoyed the night-time vision of the park as much, for the blacks and whites of the trees and marble bridges were not as vivid as in the daylight, and the gray palette of the monotonous evening always made him weary. Every now and then the Count would mutter disapproving sounds, giving a tick to the leash as if to signal Shimoni to unspoken action. It was a strange habit, and he wondered if the Count would turn into a man like those he sometimes saw twitching and wavering along the *Corso*, making indistinguishable noises to themselves.

But, at the moment, Shimoni had no idea what might amend the Count's bellicose behavior and no great desire to experiment. The lump in his belly would not retreat and by the time they had made the very long walk to the *Colosseum* and back he felt quite uncomfortable. His only desire was to seek the warmth beneath the soft cover of his Contessa's bed and try to sleep off an unfortunate exposure to a treat that had apparently gone off.

The next morning he felt no better. In fact, the lump now lay firmly a bit aft of his stomach, which he was sure would never again be satisfied, for the thought of food held no appeal. Even though the Contessa was back in full command of his leash, he was not at all excited at the prospect of greeting the other dogs at the *Pincio*. The thought of gamboling with the others frankly worried him, as it was the previous tumble that seemed to be causing his complaint. But he rallied enough to brush his tongue across the cheek of his Contessa as she carried him in the elevator, managing to coax her into keeping him in her arms all the way across the Corso and up the pitted marble staircase leading to the park.

As she placed him gently on the dewy grass he caught the faint scent of the Count, sweet tobacco on the fresh morning breeze as it swung up the hill, and turned to see him standing just behind a vendor of things Shimoni loved to chew. He thought it odd that the Count did not approach them, but then the Count had been acting in an anomalous manner ever since Shimoni had stolen his treat. Perhaps he had come to meet the Rose Woman. Perhaps she and his Contessa could finally meet.

But, as the Count began to fall farther behind, Shimoni preferred to ignore the peculiar straggler, turning away instead to concentrate on business. He sniffed the odor of a fresh trace from an unfamiliar dog, inspiring him to believe that perhaps morning duties would allay his discomfort. However, when he and his Contessa crossed the

Borghese garden and back again with nothing to report but the success of other dogs, Shimoni began to consider his situation serious.

By the time they reached the edge of the *Pincio*, the Count was still skulking behind them, just far enough to blend, unnoticed by the Contessa, into the gathering populace heading for work. But Shimoni paid no attention. He was in too much pain and occasionally, when the leash became taut and he lagged behind, his Contessa would have to stop and entice him with a soothing voice.

Finally, at the top of the path that led the way home, before he could even reach the comfort of the soft grass to the side, his belly ached in such a way that he was forced to lie prone on the sharp gravel for relief. He knew this sudden turn of events would alarm his Contessa, but he could go no further. Realizing his distress, she made some quiet, comforting sounds, knelt beside him and laid her warm gloved hand on his side. As he gave her a sideways glance she carefully lifted him into the crux of her arm and tucked him beneath her coat. The last thing he remembered was the earthy scent of the spray she used every morning, the warmth of her body and the flood of agony that carried him away to sleep.

When Shimoni awakened he was cold and confused and his belly burned. He raised his head to look through the bars of a small cage at the outline of a strange man in a white coat who held a small brown box. It was similar to the type of package that Shimoni liked to shred when slipped through the slot in the front door to his apartment, and for a moment he thought he was back in his home, awakening from a most unpleasant dream. He raised his nose and sniffed the air trying to gain a clue to the man, the package and his milieu, but the sterile atmosphere offered no answers. Groggy, he began to get to his feet but the movement yielded a sharp pain at his mid-section. He looked through a dizzy haze at his belly. Seeing it bound by a white rag resigning him to immobility, he commenced instead a visual inspection of his surroundings.

A shiny table stood in the center of a white room lighted so brightly he had to squint his eyes against the glow. Several mirrors hung on the walls around the room reflecting the image of the man in all directions. Shimoni blinked the figure into singular focus as the man began to make a soothing sound, opened the cage and slid his hand inside. He brushed his warm palm across Shimoni's head and down his neck, pausing to scratch in the exact place under his chin that gave the most pleasure. Shimoni let his tired head rest heavy on the man's hand, his eyes close and his concentration center on the affection instead of his discomfort when he heard the distant muddle of familiar voices.

He opened his eyes to see his Contessa and the Count pass through the swinging door at the end of the room and walk toward him. He could not contain his tail even though the wagging caused him pain, and when his Contessa reached inside the cage, Shimoni automatically got to his feet despite his distress. When he arrived in her arms he felt safe again, and warm, and the pain no longer mattered. Nothing mattered to him but that he was with his Contessa.

Then the man in the white coat stepped forward passing the small brown box to the Count. The Count held it as gingerly as he had the fallen pastry, placing it into the hand of the Contessa, and when he removed the cover, something happened that Shimoni had not seen in a long time. Tears began to fall from the eyes of his Contessa and onto Shimoni's head. They dripped over his forehead and down into his eyes and when they reached the corners of his mouth he caught them with his tongue, savoring their salty taste. His Contessa turned toward the Count, addressing him in the same mild tone she usually reserved for Shimoni when she found him especially smart or charming.

The Count wrapped his arms around them both,

kissed his Contessa on the cheek and gave a cursory tousle to the hair on Shimoni's head. When his Contessa rested her hand on Shimoni's side, his eyes caught a brilliant flash of light that shot across the room and scattered into a dance of tiny dots on the ceiling above. He could see that the dancing light came from a clear bit of icy looking rock that rested freshly on his Contessa's hand.

The rock was just a bit smaller than the pastry he'd eaten, certainly smaller than the type Shimoni liked to safely carry in his mouth. He understood only a foolish dog would mouth a rock that might slip carelessly down the throat, though its sparkle was indeed attractive, glittering like the waters of a Roman fountain on a summer day.

As he mused about the cool feeling such a small rock might bring to his warm mouth he caught the eye of his Contessa. Seeing that the sparkle of the rock had somehow returned the sparkle to her eyes, he was delighted. Perhaps the glitter would lead her to dare the splendid anarchy of the Roman traffic and she would rush with him across the *Corso*, sharing the exhilaration of safe passage.

Buoyed by this possibility but growing uncomfortable at the closeness of the continued embrace, Shimoni wiggled his head under his Contessa's arm. He poked his nose far enough beyond her waist for his eyes to glimpse her face in the opposite mirror as she regarded the Count, unnoticed. The Count's face reflected a stoic countenance from the opposing mirror across the stark room until his eyes met Shimoni's and his expression darkened. Even a simple-minded dog would see that dour look, neither smart nor charming, betrayed a certain displeasure and Shimoni was immediately confused by the grim reflection.

The gifts he had seen the Count give the Rose Woman always brought a pleasant appearance to the Count's face. And he rewarded her often, though Shimoni never understood the reason for the reparation. It was true, she was most pleasant and enchanting, with an easy laugh and ready treats. But as far as Shimoni could determine, these were her only amusing behaviors and, frankly, not nearly as impressive as the more sophisticated activities which he often employed to entertain his Contessa.

Indeed, the Count always seemed pleased when compensating the Rose Woman for hidden tricks and fine behavior, delighting in the sparkle small gifts brought to her eyes. Certainly the Count would notice the bright sparkle had returned to the eyes of his Contessa, Shimoni thought. Surely this, too, should make him smile.

Yet the Count's expression now reminded Shimoni more clearly of those times he had taken a toy not intended for him: a fine soft leather shoe or piece of silky clothing. Indeed the Count seemed most unhappy that his Contessa had hold of this gift, as though it should not be in her possession for it did not belong to her. And with this reflection came Shimoni's first glimmer of insight into *le sofferenze:* the sufferings of love.

His Contessa straightened, pushing back from the embrace, the little jewels of her silent stare firing into the eyes of the Count. Shimoni looked up in time to catch a final tear as it slipped from her narrowed eyes and splashed onto his quivering whiskers.

And it was then he realized he could never enjoy the company of the Rose Woman again.

Angel on a Bicycle

by Judith K. Clements

I am a fifty-eight-year-old woman sitting alone at an espresso bar on the *Campo Di Fiori* in Rome and I miss my mother. I'm here on a task: to attend to what is around me and allow the spark of inspiration to ignite my writing. I sit with my cappuccino and nothing sparks inspiration. Nothing about writing interests me. I only miss my mother, whose death was two years ago this month. I want to tell her that I'm in Italy; Mom, I'm in Italy, on a cobblestone piazza with flower stalls and fruit and vegetable stalls. Tightness pulls at my throat and I sip my cappuccino. No, I don't want to tell her about it; I want her here with me to show my mother the piazza, the flowers, the fruits, the vegetables, the fountain. She would say, "Isn't that beautiful?" And she would mean everything. Life. Isn't life beautiful?

I gaze at the people walking by the espresso bar. I am not seeing anything beautiful. Some women have gruesome dried-blood-red hair, and many wear leather jackets and high-heeled shoes, walking as if they were in their own movie, gazing at themselves. I feel the hard edge of their lives. The older women—the women my age—are stout, wear black skirts and jackets, thick flat-soled shoes, have sculpted hair, and move with a slow, stiff osteoporosis bent. Most of them go in and out the *farmacia* across the way, probably seeking relief from pain. A man my age shuffles by, a man with wild hair and unshaven face.

Wearing a dirty blue suit, he's alternately mumbling and then shouting curses of recrimination, the timeless and apparently international anthem of the alcoholic. A woman dressed in scarves and orange velvet trots beside a well-groomed man with a white handkerchief in his suit pocket, and she thrusts a plastic cup in front of him, gesturing, begging with angry entitlement and when he shakes his head she turns, glowering.

I tuck more closely into the corner of the bar, so that a potted cactus blocks half my view. I consider ordering a second cappuccino, thinking that if I get enough caffeine perhaps I won't miss my mother; I won't feel like crying in this piazza in Italy. The caffeine will jolt me past this black hole. Perhaps then I can think of something to write. Instead I remember sitting on my mother's hospital bed, holding her hand as she drifted in and out of sleep, the oxygen machine turned off, the tubes removed, her asthmatic breath no longer gurgling and labored, but finally, with the mercy of morphine, at peace.

A movement catches my eye, pulling me out of remembered experience. It is the movement of a young woman, perhaps in her twenties, riding a bicycle past the espresso bar. Her long hair is in two braids; she wears a white wooly jacket and flowing pants and she sits so gracefully on the bicycle, she rides through the crowd so spiritedly with such wide open eyes and a Mona Lisa smile, that I feel happiness. Like someone has just handed me a lovely red balloon. And when the woman on the bicycle is gone, I see the piazza with different eyes. In the market one person chooses bright oranges, another considers the many salad greens. There are pots of herbs: rosemary, parsley, oregano, basil. A young man strolls along eating strawberries from a small basket.

I pay for my cappuccino and leave the espresso bar, taking pen and journal. I watch as an old woman pares an artichoke; she is paring all the leaves of the artichoke down to its heart. I remember the Pieta I gazed at in the Vatican yesterday: the woman sculpted in the strength of stone, the mother, giving away everything, leaving only her heart, leaving only love.

Seconds before she died, my mother looked at me ablaze with love, a love I felt wrapped in and released by at the same time.

I sit now in *Campo di Fiori* on the steps below the statue of some famous person and watch a little boy in yellow pants and a blue sweater, a toddler, reach for the banana his mother purchases from the fruit stand. She peels and breaks the banana in half for him. I watch his eager eyes and black curly hair; he reminds me of my own son. One hand clutches his mother's skirt for balance, the other reaches for the banana and I sense the dance of joy vibrating throughout his body when he grasps the banana, mashing it to his lips. Ah! I taste the sweet fruit in my own mouth; feel warm cobblestones beneath my feet, with mother close by, and the sun shining. What else is there at this moment?

Isn't it beautiful?

Change

by Christopher Sirmons Haviland

Peter woke with a start, cold cobblestones poking into his back. Morning had finally arrived, and his stomach felt like birds had been pecking at it from the inside. He scratched his scraggly gray beard and pushed himself up against the old concrete wall of the café. He could tell by the light that it was still very early.

His wool blanket was getting smelly. He peered around a corner at the square. Nobody was around. He'd have to wash his blanket in the fountain before anybody came out to open their stores. The owner of the café would give him some fresh bread when she came in, but the other merchants were not so kind. They would chase him out of the square on sight.

He wrestled with his dirty jeans and began to take his morning leak into the sewer grate. His plans today were routine, as they had been for thirty years. But he mentally traced his steps anyway—what restaurant to solicit, which corner to stand, what time of day to hit up the tourists and how to do it. It was not necessary for him to commit so much thought to this, he could do it in his sleep. But he had to exercise what remained of his mind or it would finish its transformation into a potato. He refused to become one of those drooling zombies that slept under the bridges, left with little more skill than to salvage spoiled food out of the trash.

His life wasn't complicated, but it had its challenges.

He was up against some tough competition—pretty young girls with sad eyes, women with infants, and whole gypsy families who worked the crowds with stunning efficiency. Once a tourist gave money to one of them, they weren't likely to give anything to a lanky old man with a few good years left in him.

There was a very slight sound out on the square, like the padding of slippers on brick. Someone was coming, and he didn't want them to see him peeing in the alley. Despite his condition there was still a certain amount of dignity he wanted to preserve for as long as he could. He quickly finished his work and crept up to the corner to peek.

There was a girl out there, on the square. She wasn't one of the merchants or locals, he had never seen her before. She was short with long blond hair, a small nose and large round blue eyes. He couldn't determine her age, but she was young. Probably in her teens. He held his breath as she stopped at the foot of the fountain stairs and looked around. She was either looking for somebody, or checking to make sure she was alone.

She seemed vaguely familiar, and there was a fleeting memory of a girl from his very distant past. He sank into that thought for a moment, remembering a different life, and the feelings of comfort and warmth and love that it gave him. He remembered joy. But only for a second, and then he was empty again.

The girl hurried up the stairs and stood on the edge of the fountain, looking up at the statue that was mounted on the central platform. It was the image of a great warrior with huge wings on his back, standing with arms folded as if guarding a treasure. Water sprayed into the air from around his feet and into the moat around him, creating the beautiful noise that Peter enjoyed sleeping to. Peter loved fountains, and so—it would seem—did this girl. For now she was kneeling before it, with her head bowed.

He watched her with fascination. She must be the

daughter of a religious tourist, but most tourists who weren't hurrying to the airport were still snuggling in their warm hotel beds at this Autumn hour. What was she doing out here all by herself?

After a minute, she lifted her head and looked around again. And then she did something even stranger. She climbed into the fountain and dropped into the water, out of view.

Peter's mouth fell open. That girl was too small for water that cold. Was she crazy? His heart started to race. He jogged out into the court and up the stairs. There was still nobody around, and the long shadows from the dawning sun still left most of the fountain in the chilly shade. He leaned over the wall and looked into the pool, which was about five feet deep. He was just in time to see her leg disappear into a tunnel in the base of the platform.

"Hey!" Peter shouted, as if she could possibly hear him. What could she be doing?

He felt the water. It was like ice. A horrid urgency sliced through him unexpectedly, and he felt impulses that would have surprised him if he had thought more clearly.

"No, no, no," he whined to himself, barely understanding why he spoke at all, "not again. Not again."

Peter had come to Rome over thirty years ago to be blessed, and instead had been cursed. He hadn't come alone, but he ended up that way. In the years that followed, he trained himself in the art of forgetting very well. Too well, for now he wasn't sure at all why he swung his legs over the side and dipped them into the frigid water. This was not part of his routine. This was madness.

"I'm coming!" he exclaimed. But who was listening? Some ghost from the past? He didn't know this girl, and she was obviously crazy. But the impulse to save her overwhelmed him, and he ignored the pain in his legs as he took a deep breath. He pushed himself off the edge and fell into the deep water. A biting chill ran through his body, but he quickly became numb.

He positioned his body so he could swim head-first into the tunnel. It was dark inside. He didn't like it one bit, but if a small girl could do it, certainly he could. He had only one thought on his mind now. He had to get her out of there. She was going to drown, or freeze to death.

He reached and pulled his body straight in. The sides of the hole were slimy with algae, and gave him a creepy feeling. He couldn't see a thing inside, so he closed his eyes to keep them from stinging. He entered as far as he could and felt around. There was a sharp turn straight down.

Where in God's name did she go, down the drain? He shoved himself downward and felt his ears compress. He opened his eyes and saw that it wasn't dark as he descended. There was a pinkish light in the water, coming from below him, and the water starting feeling warmer. In fact it was getting easier to move on, not harder. But he needed air again, and fast.

Driven by the need to breathe, he pushed himself down until the pipe opened into a huge cavity, like a swimming pool. He could see a surface to the water not far away. He wasn't sure how this could be, but there wasn't time to work it out. He paddled for hope of air.

He broke the surface and gasped, his voice echoing in a huge chamber of pink light. He quickly found the side of the pool and pulled himself out of the water onto a tiled floor, but it wasn't cold here. In fact he wouldn't have minded staying in the water a few minutes longer to clean himself, but fear drove him to stand quickly and look about. He panted for a minute but regained his strength.

He had seen parts of Rome few people knew existed, but somehow this escaped him—and the rest of the homeless, he was sure. Word of a secret shelter under the city with clean warm water would have gotten around his community like Treasure Island.

And the room was well decorated. It was surrounded by fluted columns and walls covered with statues and words etched in some language that didn't use Latin letters. There was a large stairway opposite the pool that led down to a pair of huge doors. It was the only other way out of the chamber. The doors were guarded by a couple of gigantic female angel statues holding scrolls.

Peter was no longer concerned about the girl he had seen. Obviously she fled down here somewhere. He began to collect his thoughts and get back on track. He had a singular mission in life and it had nothing to do with exploration.

Focus, Peter, he thought to himself. *Remember who you are.*

There were voices coming from beyond the doors at the bottom of the stairwell, like a large crowd.

People untapped by competition. But who could be down here?

Shaking the cold water off, he squeaked down the stairs and gripped one of the lion-headed door handles. He found that the door pulled open easily despite its size. A warm white light flooded over him and he stood in the door and gaped in awe at the sight beyond.

He was on a balcony overlooking a depot of some kind, populated with men and women bearing large white wings on their backs. Some of them wore normal clothing—suits, dresses, casual clothes, all with holes to accommodate their wings. Others wore exotic costumes and uniforms of many styles and colors, and Peter couldn't guess what culture or time they represented. They stood in lines in front of ticket windows, crossed back and forth on a beautiful marble floor, and loitered in groups with curious feathered luggage.

Strange clocks were situated between display boards on the walls with writing in unfamiliar languages, and the ceiling was an incredible mural that looked like a complex navigational map. There were other doors and arches into greater rooms all around. Beams of yellow light cast down from high windows as if there were a sun in every direction. Yet they were too far underground and it was too early in the morning for there to be any sun at all.

Peter scratched his beard in complete wonder, tears filling his eyes. It was all so much for his failing brain to absorb.

And then he spotted the girl he had followed. She now had beautiful white feathered wings like the others, and she was talking with someone in the center of the depot. When she finished the conversation and turned back toward the stage where Peter stood, she noticed him and skidded to a halt. Peter thought of running, but these people didn't seem to present any danger. He couldn't fathom why they were all dressed in angel costumes, and he refused to entertain the notion that maybe they were *real* angels, but whatever they were they looked harmless enough.

The girl slapped a hand over her mouth in astonishment. Feeling a little self-conscious about this dramatic reaction, Peter glanced down at himself and realized he had left his zipper wide open.

He spun around and tried to close it, but the thing was stuck. He couldn't be seen this way. He might be homeless but he couldn't look like one of those degenerates. This was so embarrassing. He pulled with all his might.

"God dammit!" he shouted at the stubborn thing.

The bustling and rumble of voices stopped so suddenly that he thought he had lost his hearing. Stunned, he quit struggling with his zipper and glanced back to see that hundreds of winged people were now staring at him in shock. The blond girl walked swiftly up the stairs onto the stage but he refused to turn around with dirty underwear puffing out of his crotch.

"Sir, did you follow me from Olahm ha-Oliphoth?"

she asked with a gasp. "From Earth, I mean? From Rome?"

Without answering, Peter slowly returned to his zipper and managed to finally close it. He smoothed his gray hair down and turned around to face the crowds. Never had so many eyes looked upon him at the same time. For three decades he was lucky if even one pair would look at him directly.

Focus, focus. Remember who you are now.

Another woman gazed at him from the bottom of the stage as if with great admiration. She was wearing an ornate headdress and flowing robes like she was some kind of queen. She reached up toward him and shut her eyes.

"His name is Kefa—Peter," the gowned woman said without opening her eyes. "He thought you would drown, Serucuth, when you entered the fountain. He therefore slid through the Altitudinal Drain by drowning himself that day." She opened her eyes and ascended the stage. "He died for you," she said.

"Forgive me, Peter," said the blond, "I am Serucuth from the Choir of Authorities, and this is the Honorable Verasua from the Choir of Cherubim. You have given your life to save me, and deserve the Blessing of Beth Din, the Crown Thrones of Judgment."

Peter had no idea what they were talking about. He didn't drown, he was breathing just fine. He felt quite normal. Even his hunger pains were gone.

Serucuth and Verasua lowered themselves to one knee before him, and so did everyone else in the entire depot who could see and hear what was happening. They were all kneeling to him! This was surreal. How could they mistake him for royalty when he was dressed like this?

"May you be anointed by Akatriel Yah Yehod Sebaoth, the Lord of Spirits, and cleansed of your transgressions by Emmanuel the Lamb. And may you sit higher than the Bene ha-Elohim for all eternity. Amen!"

"Amen!" repeated the crowds in thunderous but perfectly harmonic unison.

Focus, focus, Peter kept repeating to himself, holding back a fart.

"Before you face the Holy Elim, what would you have of us, Peter of Rome?" Serucuth asked from her knee.

The girl's blue eyes were focused clearly on his face, looking through his scraggly beard and dirty skin as if none of that mattered. He felt special for the first time since…

Focus!

His mind cleared again, and he held onto it this time. He took a deep breath, reached his hand toward Serucuth with restored resolve, and went to work.

"Spare change?"

Torn

by Kathleen Antrim

John McCord slammed the screen door behind him, nearly knocking it from the hinges. He took the porch steps two at a time, heading for his old Ford pickup. He climbed behind the wheel, a spring creaking in protest as the bench seat gave under his sturdy frame.

The box in the front pocket of his blue jeans dug into his thigh, the pinch a welcome distraction from his raw confusion. He rolled down the window and gunned the engine. The truck roared to life. Sunlight glinted off the blond hair of his tanned forearm as he propped his elbow on the door.

He drove past the church, then twice around the block, wondering at his stupidity. Finally he pulled to a stop under a large, budding elm across the street from the church grounds. On this clear spring morning, lawn mowers hummed and the smell of freshly cut grass floated on the breeze. His thoughts were drawn back to afternoon picnics in the summer sun along the riverbank with her. Over time, the soothing sound of running water mixed with laughter became their song, one he wistfully danced to in his mind's eye as he thought of her. Her smile. Her laugh. Her love.

He watched a long white limousine wind its way up the driveway and then park in front of the steps that led to two huge mahogany doors. The white steeple stood tall and proud above the church entrance, proclaiming by its existence faith, hope, and love. Spiritual aspects, John knew, that were lacking in his life, for he'd never been one to make time for prayer, or for God. If he'd bothered to pray, he wondered, would his life be different? His choices altered?

Unable to stop himself, he turned off the ignition and stepped from the truck. The limousine door opened, and her veil appeared.

She turned in his direction, then hesitated for a moment.

His breath caught. Had she seen him? Could he bear it if she had? His cheeks flushed. If he'd been closer, would he have seen pity in her eyes? Anger? Or love? Instinctively, he reached into his pocket to grasp the small box. A secret she never knew. A question never asked.

She floated up the steps to the looming mahogany doors and another man waiting inside. Bridesmaids followed in the wake of her laughter. He could feel another piece of his heart shatter against his ribs, the pain tangible and permanent. John knew that she was the measure by which all others would be weighed and found lacking.

He felt the church as if it were alive, its pull urgent and demanding. Yet he fought back, willing himself to stillness. What right did he have to tamper with her decision? She had moved on, and he'd forfeited his chance to stand beside her at the altar. He grasped the box tightly.

Pride, desire, and a fear of rejection warred within him. He took a deep breath, leaned against the pickup, and crossed his arms over his broad chest. Waiting. But for what?

Guests crowded the entrance. Their excited chatter felt like a warning against his vigil.

The chauffeur lounged near the steps, smoking a cigarette.

Without moving, John could imagine the scene inside. Bright stained glass throwing rays of color across the altar, flowers scenting the air, and her radiant smile holding everyone's attention. The agony of the unspoken finally pushed him toward the church. Could he right this wrong?

He pictured himself bursting through the doors. All eyes pulled from the altar to stare at his intrusion. The shock in her eyes turned to love as he reached out to her. He straightened from the truck and took a step toward her, the church, and life.

"Hey, watch it." A cyclist swerved around him.

John retreated into himself. He'd thought that marriage was more than he could handle, but he'd been wrong. Never knowing what could have been was the true demon.

The chauffeur lit another smoke. How many was that? John wondered.

He glanced at his watch, unable to discern how long he'd been standing there. How long they'd been in the church. He couldn't bear to stay, yet he couldn't force himself to leave.

The roaring thunder of the church bells reverberated through him. His knees buckled. John steadied himself against the Ford.

The chauffeur tossed his cigarette onto the concrete.

John watched as he ground the butt under his heel, the assault somehow personal.

After a moment John climbed into the pickup. Tears ran unchecked down his cheeks. Only the searing pain in his chest registered. He threw the truck into gear. Rubber melted onto blacktop as he peeled out, tire tracks the only evidence of his presence.

When the church bells rang out the eleventh hour, she stood in the vestibule of the church. Her bridesmaids waited around her, but she felt alone. Chords from the wedding march filled the church. A proud smile on his face, her father stepped toward her and offered his arm. She knew that he'd mortgaged everything for this day, this union, a chance for his only child to marry out of a life of struggle.

She glanced at her engagement ring, the fit suddenly tight and uncomfortable. Her hands began to shake. Thoughts raced through her mind, challenging all that this day represented.

John had come for her. She'd glimpsed his truck, blond hair, loving eyes. She grew faint. Confusion swirled around her, crystallizing in a truth she could no longer avoid. She closed her eyes and swallowed hard. What made her think she could ever get over him?

She tried to summon all of the reasons why she'd agreed to marry another, but what once seemed so responsible, so logical now felt like folly. A life to be built on lies.

John drove aimlessly, his destination once certain now clouded with remorse and self-doubt. The river called. He parked his old Ford on the deserted bridge that overlooked their secret place. The place where they'd cuddled together in the back of his truck, counting the falling stars and dreaming of the future. Here life had been wrapped in her love, tied up with a ribbon of hope and promise.

John stepped out of the pickup. The sun was full upon the day, warming his broad shoulders and soothing muscles worn by manual labor. He moved to the railing and stared down into the turbulent water below. Pregnant with a late mountain thaw, the river had grown swollen upon the banks. Currents teemed beneath him.

With callused hands, he pulled the small box from his pocket, then snapped open the lid. Sunlight caught the facets of the diamond, magnifying its cut and perfection. He thought of the jeweler's enthusiasm for his selection, and the wave of optimism that had carried him toward making a commitment. But he'd lacked the ability to follow through, to reach out and grab what he so desperately wanted, needed. His courage was submerged in a tide of indecision and anxiety.

The box dropped as he pulled the ring from its grip. He turned it from side to side, the rays cutting across his face and chest. Thoughts lacerated his mind as he examined the promise never spoken. A proposal he couldn't make for fear of the freedom he'd have to relinquish, and the vulnerability he'd have to risk. The irony was not lost on him, for he was forever bound to her by love, and the bite of vulnerability gripped him savagely.

John climbed back into the truck. Through the open window, he stared at the steely river, cold and unyielding. He cocked his arm, tempted to let the ring fly, to watch the sparkle hit the water, then vanish into the inky depths, as if by this very act he'd banish the pain. But suddenly he realized that heartbreak like his had no cure, for he'd caused his own loss. The full weight of this truth fell upon him. With his foot, he punched the accelerator.

The engine roared.

He threw the gears into drive.

The wheels screamed. The old pickup bolted through the rail.

The ring flew from his grasp as he plummeted into the murky waters.

As she looked up the aisle, the guests stared back in happy anticipation. Her groom and a prosperous future waited at the altar. She turned to her father and their gaze locked.

Joy and pride slipped from his expression, replaced by confusion and pain. He shook his head in disbelief.

Tears filled her eyes and blurred his image; no words would come.

She dropped her bouquet. Rose petals scattered at her feet. Running from the church, she tore the veil from her head. She dashed down the steps, across the lawn, and out to the street. With all of her might, she ran from her mistake, finally certain that her heart and her future belonged with John.

Chest heaving, she stood between the tracks left by

his tires. Silence draped the street like a cloak of despair. She spun on her heel, searching for his truck, for him. The man she loved.

She called his name softly, then again and again, her voice escalating in volume and fear.

The street echoed a hollow note in return.

In the silence, his pain enveloped her. Arms wrapped across her waist, she doubled over at the intensity. Suddenly she understood. He was lost to her forever.

A keen of anguish, long and low, ripped through the air. She dropped to her knees.

A siren wailed in the distance.

Frustration with a Capital F
by David Nutt

Standing at one end of the *Campo di Fiori*, he heard the clear-pitched sound of a soprano's voice mingled with the elegant chords of a violin coming from a passageway to his left. Even to his uneducated musical ear, he knew the performers were striving to reach a high level of perfection. The haunting sounds drove him to explore the passageway. The first thing he noticed, opposite the house where the music was coming from, was a dirty old mattress lying in the gutter. This ugly sight seemed alien to the sounds of music wafting through the passageway. He looked across the narrow street, hoping to see who was performing. The windows were wide open: violin playing on the first floor, operatic singing on the second floor. He stepped back to get a better view when, to his surprise, a violin came flying out of the first floor window. It fell with a thud into the center of the mattress. The singer's voice from the second floor still pervaded the passageway as if nothing had happened; there was complete silence from the first floor. He bent down, picked up the violin and shouted up towards the first floor windows.

"This yours?"

A head popped out. "It was until a few seconds ago."

"Want it back?"

"Sure, why not? It will save me the bother of coming down later to retrieve it. Come on up."

The door on the first floor opened to reveal a small old man dressed in evening clothes. He had a long pale face supporting an elegant little goat's beard, but it was his sparkling eyes, full of youth and enthusiasm that told his visitor he was no ordinary man. As he took the violin, he introduced himself as Alberto.

"Please come in."

His visitor introduced himself as George. Without more fuss, George was ushered into the large room overlooking the street. On entering, George caught his breath in amazement. The room was divided carefully down the middle into two distinct sections: one for music, and one for painting. On the musical side, the walls were fully furnished with violins in different stages of repair. They hung from floor to ceiling like a regiment of soldiers on a drill square. He turned to the painting side. Here the walls were covered with canvases, many of the pictures half finished, some had just been started, paint tubes and brushes cluttered the floor.

"You also paint!" exclaimed George.

"Today we only talk about music," the old man replied. "Only music."

Not being a musician, George was not sure how to continue the conversation, but out of politeness to his host he turned his attention to the violin wall. The obvious topic of conversation came to his lips. "May I ask why you threw the violin out of the window?"

"Frustration." The old man replied looking towards to the violin wall. "Frustration!"

"Why frustration?" questioned George.

"Ah! It's a long story. As you see I am old, and slowly I am beginning to forget how it all started." He stopped a minute as if losing his train of thought. Then he took George by the arm and said. "My friend, you are in Rome. Everybody here thinks they are great artists; singers think they are Caruso, painters Leonardo da Vinci, composers, Puccini, and so it goes on! Our desire to imitate our great artists is unlimited. We are crazy! I am Italian, crazy like the rest of them."

He paused to allow George to understand the true Italian artistic meaning of crazy.

"At one time I was a well-known violinist—world concert tours and all the trappings. In all due modesty I know how to play the violin. You ask me why I threw the violin out of the window? You see, my friend, many years ago in Naples I heard a street musician reach a note with his violin that I had never heard before and have never heard since. After that, I have been trying to find that note. Sometimes I get very close but it still eludes me. At first I thought it was my playing; then I thought it was the violin; as you can see I have tested a fair number. In frustration I started throwing the violins out of the window. It got quite expensive so that is why I have put a mattress there. Ah! It's crazy; but what can we do? Listen to my wife singing."

He pointed his finger at the ceiling and paused to allow George to listen.

"You hear her, my friend? She is smitten with the same bug. Once my wife heard a great operatic soprano, like herself, reach a note so high and of such vocal beauty that she just had to try to copy it. Her attempts have been going on for years, but unlike me she cannot just throw her voice out of the window. She has to live with her frustration. George, my friend, take my advice: if you get frustrated just throw out whatever gets in your way. It helps."

They talked on for a while, George mostly listening. Finally he saw that the old man was tired. As he said good-bye, he noticed that all the paintings on the walls were on the same subject in various stages of progression. He was about to say something but remembered the old man's words "Today we talk only about music."

George didn't sleep well that night; two recurring thoughts disturbed him. First, what could he throw out of his life that was getting in the way? And second, what was the meaning of all those pictures? The next day at noon he was back in the *Campo de Fiori*. He immediately heard the haunting voice of the soprano but the violin was silent. He crept down the passageway to see if there was a violin on the mattress. To his great amusement he saw paintbrushes being thrown out of the first floor window.

Over the coming months George often thought about his meeting with the old man and slowly began teaching himself to open his windows and throw things out.

It must have been six months later at eleven o'clock in the morning when George's British Airways flight from London touched down at the Rome Airport.

"*Campo di Fiori*, please."

As he alighted from the taxi, he could hear no singing, no violin. He went straight to the passageway. No mattress. The house was boarded up. As he stood gazing up at the first and second floor, a man came out of a door further down the passage.

"Please," George said, pointing to the house, "do you know where the old man has gone?"

The passerby looked at him. "The soprano! She threw herself out of the second floor window. They were artists, crazy people."

George wasn't so sure....

One Night Stand

by Elva Adams

Hazel Cornelius rounded the corner of the piazza *Campo Di Fiori* looking for a sign that would help her find an overnight accommodation. She had toured Rome all day and the constant pounding on the cobblestone streets made the soles of her feet throb and beg for relief. Her penny loafers felt like they were three sizes too small. She questioned what she was thinking when she strayed from her tour group in order to explore the side streets of this vast city. However, she promised herself that when she retired, she would loosen up and do the things she was not allowed to do when her mother had been alive.

As dusk blanketed the market square, a gray building streaked with black and rust-colored crevices captured her attention. The façade of the picturesque hostel was something one would see on a postcard, inviting and appealing to the eye, complete with closed burgundy shutters. Looking up at the wall covered to the eaves with a mix of lavender and white wisteria, Hazel immediately thought about her mother.

Hazel, when you go out today, please pick up some wisteria so I can enjoy the fragrance while I get ready for bed.

Yes, mother. White or lavender?

Hazel, dear, you're fifty-five years old. Haven't you learned how to form a complete sentence yet? No one would ever guess you taught English for twenty-seven years!

Mother, do you want the white wisteria or do you want the lavender wisteria for your bedroom?

Ah, that's more like it, Hazel. I would like a mix of white wisteria and lavender wisteria.

Why is this old woman bothering me? Ever since daddy died a few years ago, she won't let me breathe. I'm almost sorry I promised him that I'd take care of her.

Hazel noticed the sign below the window box, Hotel Abalone, and decided to inquire about a room. She thought that perhaps the hotel was not open, given the closed shutters. The double door, black with huge brass knockers, displayed a small sign, barely visible, "Welcome." As she lifted one of the knockers, an old man about seventy, gray hair pulled back in a pony tail, opened the door.

"*Buona sera, signora.*"

"Oh hello, *signore. Parla inglese?*"

"*Si signora. Americana?*"

"Why yes. *Si.* I need a room. One night." He took her bag.

"Yes, come in. You must register, please. *Scusa signora.* Vittorio, come please. We have a new guest joining us this evening."

Hazel was filling out the registration card so she paid little attention to the man who appeared at her side. The scent of a spicy cologne floating toward her nostrils made her weaken. *That smells like daddy's favorite.*

"*Buona sera, signora.* I am Vittorio. Welcome to Hotel Abalone. You will enjoy your stay. I guarantee." Lowering his head to meet her hand, he placed it between his, slowly kissed the outside of her hand, then turned it upward while his tongue briefly licked the inside of her palm so delicately that it sent shivers up and down her entire body.

"Hello, Vittorio. I'm Hazel Cornelius." She waited for him to stand erect so she could see his face. *Oh, my goodness. Be still my heart.* She could barely move. Hazel was now looking directly into the piercing black eyes of a man in his thirties. Wavy black hair cascaded down and around his shoulders, a widow's peak appeared to dive into his forehead, and a pencil thin mustache balanced itself over full cherry lips.

"May I take your bag, *signora?*"

"No, it's okay. It's only a..."

"*Signora*, permit me please," he said as he firmly took hold of the bag. Vittorio led her to a set of lavishly polished cherrywood steps. "One flight up, *signora*. The best room in the house only for you. Visiting *Roma* from where?"

"Oh, I live in Iowa. I just retired from teaching and am on vacation for a month. Rome is my first stop."

Vittorio stopped at a room with the number seven set in black enamel and adorned with a brass plate. He stood in front of it as the wooden door gradually slid open.

Hazel's jaw dropped in amazement. "How did you do that?"

"Oh, the room is *senziente*, or alive, for you, *signora*. It was waiting for your arrival. Here, take this key in the event it does not operate."

"Ouch! The key, it stabbed me."

"You're bleeding. Here let me have your finger."

Vittorio gently placed Hazel's middle right hand finger in his mouth and sucked it tenderly. He tugged and pulled on it, all the while staring at her. "*Signora*, you have most beautiful, oh how you say, hazel eyes, and pretty silver hair I have seen in long time." Hazel quickly pulled her hand away.

"Thank you, Vittorio. I think my finger stopped bleeding." Hazel was aware that her underwear was suddenly sticking to her. She felt a titillating energy unlike any she had ever felt. She noticed, too, that her nipples, which were neatly and perfectly held in place by her Maidenform brassiere, were standing at attention. For a fleeting second, she envisioned him stroking them.

"Well, *signora*, please to ring desk if you need anything. Dinner will be sent to your room in maybe one hour, yes? You take warm bath and put on the robe in closet."

"Thank you, Vittorio." Hazel closed the door, an embarrassed smile coyly enveloping her lips. She was barely aware that she was sucking on the finger Vittorio had put in his mouth.

Hazel's chest felt alive and so did her lower body. She ran a warm bath, quickly removed her plus-sized black slacks, pink overblouse, bra and sticky panties, and slipped into the tub. She closed her eyes and imagined Vittorio's tongue licking the inside of her hand and sucking on her finger. The longing in her forced her hand to slide down into the warm soapy water and between her thighs as she gently rubbed herself to the point of release. She let out a sigh and lightly soaped herself, enjoying the tingling sensation that repeated itself over and over again. Rinsing her body, she felt a gnawing regret at having to gratify herself.

A knock on the bathroom door interrupted her thoughts. "Yes, who is it?"

"It is Vittorio. Dinner is served." He was in the room! She quickly grabbed a towel and got out of the bathtub.

"Okay, please leave it. I'll be right out." Hazel heard the door close and stepped into the room. A small table with a lavender tablecloth was positioned in front of the queen- sized bed. There was a miniature spray of white and lavender wisteria in a tiny white vase. *I wonder if mother knows what I did.* She put on the robe which was spread out on the bed and sat down to eat a meal of freshly baked trout, small parsleyed red potatoes, and green vegetables sautéed in garlic and oil. She made some tea, drank half a cup, and became very sleepy. She lay back on the unmade bed and felt her eyes flutter before they closed.

"*Signora*, wake up." Hazel heard the whisper, but she was drowsy. She lifted her head slightly and imagined that she saw Vittorio's face peeking up at her from between her legs, her robe slightly open, and falling away on either side. She dared not move as wave upon wave of delicious ecstasy overtook her. She felt a pleasure never before experienced. Hazel's eyes closed, and strangely enough her thoughts were to *eat, drink and be merry because for me, tomorrow might not come.*

Suddenly, Hazel's eyes opened. She felt like someone was watching her. She was now naked and neatly placed under the covers. How did she get like this? She felt shame and guilt. What was happening to her? She got up, grabbing her robe as she went into the bathroom. She ran cool water and began splashing her face with it. She raised herself up, turned and caught a glimpse of her face in the mirror when she sensed someone, or something gently pass by and brush against her chest. The air was filled with the scent of allspice. Someone was in the room. "Daddy, is that you?"

"Don't scream, *signora*. I hear you yell from next room, and I come to see if you are okay."

It was Vittorio, but how, *when* did he come into the room? And he had no clothes on.

"I sleep naked, please to forgive. I was afraid to waste time. I go now if you are safe."

"Yes, I'm fine," said Hazel, averting her eyes as she gathered her robe to cover her own nakedness.

"I'm sorry if I scare you." He took her hand in his, turned the palm toward him, and again kissed and licked it playfully with his tongue. Hazel let out a moan.

"*Signora*, please don't be afraid. Vittorio stay with you, help you."

"No, Vittorio, it's not necessary. Please go." She wanted him to stay. No, to go.

"As you wish." He came toward her and embraced her so tenderly that she melted into his arms. He placed his lips on her mouth, his tongue darting in and out leaving Hazel breathless and unable to do anything but groan softly. He ran his fingers playfully over her breasts, lightly kissing her nipples. Hazel's breath stopped as Vittorio licked all the way up to her neck. Placing his mouth under her right ear, he sucked softly, yet tenderly, on her neck. By now she was moaning. Vittorio continued sucking but now more firmly, harder.

"Vittorio, you're hurting me. Please don't."

"Please not to worry. Vittorio will not harm you."

He drove his sharp teeth into the softness of her neck. She let out a cry—the pain was excruciating. As silence followed, he said, "*Signora*, you are so beautiful. Vittorio did not hurt you?"

He cupped her cheeks in his hands and looked into Hazel's face as she timidly batted her eyes at him. He carried her to the bed, laid her down, and continued to suckle her, make love to her, draw from her as she moaned over and over again.

The next morning, Hazel awakened to the aroma of freshly brewed coffee and bacon and eggs. Breakfast awaited her in the dimly lit alcove opposite her bed, but she noticed that the lock was secured inside the room. *How strange.* She went into the bathroom and stared at her face which appeared pale, her eyes darkened by circles. Hazel began to feel a newfound energy. She noticed the presence of two red pin-sized holes on the right side of her neck. She called down to the desk.

"*Buon giorno, signore.* May I please speak to Vittorio?"

"*Buona mattina, signora.* You say Vittorio?"

"Yes, he told me to ring the desk if I needed anything."

"*Scusa,* but when he say that, *signora?*"

"Yesterday evening when I arrived. After he brought me to my room."

"Just a minute, *signora.*" Hazel heard a muffled sound as though the clerk put his hand over the receiver to talk to someone.

"Hello?"

"Yes, *signora.* Will you be checking out?"

"Yes, I will be checking out *pronto.* But first I would like to speak to Vittorio."

"Yes, I know, *signora*. But please to come down to the lobby first. My name is Aldo."

"Very well, I will come down now."

"I prepare your bill."

Hazel was troubled. She sat on the bed trying to make sense of what she was feeling. She blinked hard and swore that for an instant, in the dimmed breakfast alcove, stood a naked Vittorio blowing kisses at her. Another blink produced nothing.

She quickly gathered her belongings into her bag and stared at the robe hanging in the closet. Hazel then stood in front of the door, which opened slowly. She stepped into the hallway, and the door closed behind her. She walked down the flight of steps and stopped at the front desk.

"Yes, *signora*. May I help you?" She did not recognize the clerk.

"I'm checking out of room seven. I would also like to speak to Vittorio. Now."

"*Signora* Cornelius, please to describe Vittorio." The clerk's furrowed brows showed concern.

"Well, he was very tall, he had black wavy hair, mustache, very handsome, dark eyes. Why?"

"*Signora*, please to look at painting there on the wall next to door."

Hazel walked over to the small graying portrait, which was smartly framed in black lacquer. Squinting her eyes, she reached into her purse to get her reading glasses.

"Well? Is this the man you call Vittorio?"

"Oh my. Why yes, that's Vittorio, but how? This picture looks old. It's almost faded."

"*Si*. That was Don Vittorio Sardonno, the great-great-grandfather of the owner of this establishment."

"Great-great-grandfather? I don't know what you mean."

"Unfortunate, the owner, he is out of town since two weeks."

"Who, Vittorio?"

"No, *signora*. The gentleman in picture *was* Vittorio. He die in the seventeenth century, I believe."

"But that can't be. He was here and real. I know. He took my hand. I don't understand. Where was Vittorio from? Where did he live when he died?"

"Don Vittorio he was born and die in Pompeii, where is the big *como se dice Montagna di Vulcano di Pompei. Signora*, are you not well?"

"This can't be. I met him. He was here, in your hotel, yesterday." Hazel was reeling from the disturbing news.

"Are you sure you are not imagining?"

"I don't know what to think. This just can't be."

Hazel gave the clerk her credit card, shakily signing the receipt. She imagined that she felt a faint brush against her right cheek, the aroma of allspice subtly dotting the air.

"*Grazie, signore*. By any chance, can you recommend a good hotel in Pompeii?"

"Why *si*. Of course. Wait here. I go get my book."

Like a feather from out of nowhere, Hazel noticed a small card drifting to the floor. Bending down, she scooped it up. She couldn't believe her eyes. The card, simple, unadorned, had two printed lines:

— *Visit the Inn at Pompeii* —
— *Compliments of Hotel Abalone* —

Leaving the Hotel Abalone and the wisteria flowers behind, a smiling Hazel stepped out into the bustling market square, savoring the thought of her future in Pompeii.

The Antique Typewriter
by Ann Klein

The old typewriter was possessed. I knew it the moment I looked through the dirt-smudged window of the antique shop. That was significant, considering I didn't believe in that sort of thing and hadn't believed in much of anything since my wife left me alone and directionless.

I had been meandering the streets of Rome for days, trying to find inspiration. I wanted to be a writer, hoped all my life to be a writer, but never had an idea worthy of starting. Failing inspiration, I headed down one of Rome's many narrow, cobbled streets looking for intrigue. I was ready to abort my efforts in favor of lunch when I spied the antique shop.

As I approached the window, I was certain I saw the keys of the ancient instrument move, independent of any fingers. The flat black keys rimmed in silver had well-worn white letters. They stopped, of course, as soon as I got my nose close enough to get a good look.

The door jangled, announcing my entry, and the elderly shopkeeper looked at me with pale blue eyes, clouded by cataracts, then looked toward the typewriter and smiled as if he had been expecting me.

My spine iced.

"You writer, *si*?" he asked as he gingerly lifted the typewriter with gnarled fingers and an unsuspected strength.

"Some people might argue that," I said and watched

as he placed it next to the cash register, amazed by his boldness.

"Cash or credit?"

"How much?"

"Does it matter?" He smiled.

I could not get out of the shop and away from the old man fast enough. With my treasure carefully wrapped and tucked under my arm, I headed straight for my hotel. I wanted to write—no, I *had* to write, as my mind flooded with stories and the chaos of ideas they brought.

I barely noticed the magnificient view of Rome when I got back to my room. I ordered room service and wolfed down tasteless food as I contemplated the empty sheet of paper I'd rolled into the machine. Moments later, I found myself sitting at the desk with no memory of going there, yet the paper was filled with words. It took several attempts to extract the sheet of paper because my hand shied away from it, as if afraid it would be stuck with a needle.

Three words were written repeatedly across and down the page: "Turn me over." I frowned as I turned the paper over, then realized that the message was to turn the typewriter. I was certain that whoever had written the words through me had been witness to my error. I had a well-developed complex about anything that made me look foolish, regardless of the audience.

I took a slow, deep breath, then lifted the typewriter and struggled to turn it over. I recalled how effortlessly the old shopkeeper had carried it and felt ashamed of my lack of upper body strength. Attached to the bottom of the instrument was a gold plate with the initials JMM. I stopped breathing.

The remainder of the day was spent with a bottle of Scotch, a telephone call to my father, and a lot of staring at the ancient typewriter. I needed the fortification once my father confirmed my hunch. The typewriter had belonged to my great-grandfather, Joseph Michael McCarthy, Jr., an ex-priest and prominent mystery writer in the forties and fifties. He was found dead in the study of his home near the Vatican in 1957, presumably of natural causes at the age of seventy-two. My granddad always insisted there had been foul play because great-granddad's beloved typewriter—now my typewriter—and the manuscript he said he had completed, were never found. The police never even investigated the missing articles.

I finished the Scotch and called room service to order another. It was going to take more reinforcements to get me through the night with a haunted typewriter.

The bright sunlight rudely pried open my eyes and my neck muscles seized in spasm. Easy chairs were not meant for sleeping. The new bottle of Scotch was empty. The pain in my temples and the cotton in my mouth confirmed that the alcohol hadn't been wasted. I glared at the typewriter, but I couldn't hate it. It wanted something from me. It had to, to have spoken to me so loudly.

Before even brushing my teeth, I felt my hands drawn to the keys. My fingers quivered momentarily in protest before being sucked to them like magnets to metal.

The remainder of the day went by in a haze. My mind sat independent of my hands and I watched with horrified fascination as page after page was typed and stacked neatly in a pile next to the typewriter. My fingers typed so fast I didn't have time to read what was being written. The cramping didn't start until the typing was finished. Three hundred and eighty-six pages into the novel, my hands fell to my lap and the words "The End" were centered on the page.

I desperately needed to sleep, but my curiosity would have no part of it. I made myself as comfortable as possible and began to read. The same magic that had fired the book was working overtime to keep me awake through the night until I had read every word.

There was no question. It was the final novel of Joseph Michael McCarthy, Jr.

I called my granddad with the news. He'd always wanted me to be a writer, said I had inherited my looks from his father, he was certain I'd inherited the writing talent as well.

He was happier that I was acknowledging the real source of the work than about the work itself. It never occurred to me to claim the book as my own, but I had to admit, my roguish past would lead anyone to that conclusion. Truth was, I would never claim credit for anything that came from that typewriter without its permission. It looked so innocent sitting on the desk, but I knew better. I was determined to establish a good working relationship with it eventually, but all that could wait until my granddad arrived in Rome.

Granddad was excellent shape for being eighty-two, but I assumed he would need to rest after an intercontinental flight. I was wrong. He came to my room before checking in. After a handshake and a hug, I lost his attention to the typewriter. He was spellbound by its presence, but unafraid. He lifted it up and looked underneath. Tears filled his eyes.

"It found you, Michael," he said. "That is synchronicity at its finest. I would like to read the manuscript now. We can talk when I'm finished."

A week earlier, I would have felt summarily dismissed, but not today. I had changed, and it was clearly a change for the better. I never knew my great-grandfather when he was living, but I was going to enjoy getting to know him now. I hoped he'd share his writing secrets. I hoped he'd show me what to do with the myriad ideas that came along with his typewriter.

Maybe we'd even collaborate on the next book.

Images: Italia
by Mary Ann Brock

O Roma!

O ancient, savage Queen

Nestled with wolves in millennium thistles,

You are eons into your reign.

With storms for your hair,

The sea for your face, and the Lazio sun for your heart,

O whom will you bless,

And whom will you knight,

And whom will you shred apart?

The Art of Imagination
by Dorothy Allison

I got off the plane in Rome looking for nuns. I couldn't help myself. Italy for me is Catholicism and big stone monasteries crammed full of mysterious romantic figures. I was raised a Baptist child and struck at an early age by the romantic figure of Audrey Hepburn, her dark eyes shining and her nun's robe a white so pure it had to have been kissed by the breath of God. Catholic friends told me horror tales about nuns—how they were actually dour faced creatures who spanked children's hands with wooden rulers and picked their teeth with dirty fingernails. But I was still enthralled with my own fantasy, convinced that nuns were separate, secret, and touched by the magical. Yes, of course they ate and spit and went to bed at an early hour, but no matter. They were a relic of the medieval, as close to the fanciful as one could get in modern life, and bound up in my mind with the black death and the lead poisoning that inevitably accompanied the creation of stained glass windows. Lives spent in service, walled away from daytime television and suburban carwashes. How could they not be heroines?

In 1998 passing through that same airport, I had seen nuns in wimples with cell phones, smoking cigarettes, sipping sweet soda and wiping their mouths with ragged yellow napkins. It was one of those moments when the romantic collides with the real and nothing remains the same. I had stood with my mouth open, staring, unabashed and rude. Nuns that smoked, nuns that shoved carts full of luggage, nuns that carried big ugly pocketbooks and frowned in my direction, I almost missed my bus following them around. I had wanted to ask them questions, lift their wimples and check to see what was hidden in those pocketbooks—though I did none of that of course. I regained my poise and just walked away from them.

This time, I told myself as I got off the plane, I won't be shocked. I will keep my sense of humor. So nuns use cell phones? So what? I gathered up my luggage and passed through customs. I would look for the van for the hotel. I wouldn't get distracted.

There was a pair of them. They were standing at a kiosk trading sips of a bottle of orange soda. One of them was punching keys on a laptop while the other wiped sweat off her eyebrows. Nuns using computers, I shook my head. The older one, the one at the keyboard, scratched her hip through the fabric of her habit. The skirt was calf length. I looked down at her thick stockings and brogan shoes. OK, a nun who used a computer and wore support hose. All right. What if they were part of a secret sect of nuns plotting to return the world to God? What if the hip scratcher was a hacker of prodigious talents, one who was finishing up the code to a virus that would bring down the world banking system? What if she and her sisters were plotting the collapse of all the multinational corporations, the return to a more ordered and Godly society. Fanatics willing to spend their lives praying and typing code, they were waiting the arrival of a South American order that would...

"Ms. Allison? Ms. Allison?" The man behind me bumped me with his cart of luggage and smiled apologetically. "Ms. Allison?"

"Yes."

"Oh! I am so glad to see you. Really looking forward to this. Wanted to ask you..." He shoved his cart up beside me, nodded happily and smiled widely. "Wanted to know how this was going to work. You know, just a hint. If there were exercises, if we were going to do them together. What you planned..." He nodded some more, looking around at the people pushing passed us. He caught a bag that was tilting off his cart and pulled it back up safely on top of the rest of the luggage.

I risked one more glance at my postmodern nuns and sighed. I realized I had been angling toward them. The back of my brain was plotting a way to check just what it was that was on that screen. No doubt it would have been in Latin, or more likely modern Italian, unintelligible to me. A map program maybe or a list of addresses. What did nuns keep on their computers?

I turned back to the eager student.

"Exercises?" I shrugged and gave my own rueful smile. "Of course." I looked around for the driver and the van, anyone else I knew or even another batch of nuns. "You're going to write," I told him. "You are going to write a lot."

"Well, I didn't really know if I should do this program." He had three suitcases, all carefully locked with little silver master locks, and a computer case with big Fragile stickers all over it. "I'm pretty close to finishing my novel, and this could be a big interruption for me. Thinking I might just hole up in my room and work."

"Mmmmm." I braked my cart, with my one suitcase and briefcase. I had brought an extra coat but wasn't sure I was going to need it. There were tiny flowers and buds all over the trees I could see through the windows. The sun looked warm.

"What do you think?"

I looked back at him. His face was wide open, his eyes bright and confident. I had seen him before, I thought, or I had seen someone like him.

"You're almost finished with your book?" I said gently.

He nodded.

"You think it's pretty good?"

"Well." He hesitated. His eyes were suddenly focused down at my feet. "Well, you know how it is." He looked back up at me. "I think it is, but how can I tell? I was hoping..."

I put my hand up. "No," I said. "No. I won't read it."

"Oh," he sighed.

"But I will read anything you write here, anything new you write here." I lifted my briefcase and wiggled it at him. It was fairly light and easy to wave in the air. "I have a novel almost finished myself, and a deadline looming. But the novel isn't in this bag. It is at home. What I am here for is what you should be here for—to start some new things, to shake out my imagination and recharge my batteries." I risked another quick glance at the kiosk. My nun was packing up. I sighed, and then realized the writing student thought it was meant at him. He looked stricken.

"Don't look like that." I pointed at my nuns. "You see them?"

He frowned. "See who?"

"The two nuns, the ones with the laptop at that kiosk."

"Oh, yes."

"What do you think they are doing here?"

He gave me a perplexed look. "I don't know. Waiting for someone maybe, or for a flight. I'm afraid I don't know much about nuns."

"Me either," I admitted happily. "But I wonder about them. And I never get a chance to let myself really look at them, or even think much about them. I was thinking here I might take the chance to take a really good look."

"To look at nuns?" He sounded confused.

"And cathedrals and buses and ice cream stands and gardens and markets and book stores and ruins and trains and I don't know, anything that catches my eye." I waved one hand at everything that surrounded us, all the people and luggage and policemen and drivers with big handwritten signs. "Going somewhere different makes me think about what I take for granted. It makes me wonder about everything. Makes me want to make notes and stare at people. Takes me right back to when I first started writing and was making up a story about everything."

"You are going to start a new novel here?" He looked surprised.

"Or a story, or a series of stories. Maybe a book about nuns." I laughed, but he didn't seem to get the joke. "I don't know what I will write," I told him. "I only know I am going to let myself feel completely free to be a writer in a city I don't know among other people who love writing as much as I do. "

"Oh." He nodded. "That's good. That's really nice."

"Yes."

My nuns stepped around us, one on either side, big pocketbook clamped under one's arm and laptop in the other one's hands. The one who had scratched her hip gave me a quick calculating glance, bright black eyes, fierce and intelligent.

"*Scusi.*"

I smiled and watched them walk away. Maybe they were meeting a plane, but maybe they were not. I'd have to make it up for myself.

Steps

by John Oglesby

The staccato beats of Maria Donnelly's heels against the cobblestones of *Piazza di Spagna* ricocheted from the storefronts and down the shopping canyons of Via Condotti. She slung the expensive shopping bag holding her new Gucci scarf over her shoulder and clipped on across the piazza, her cell phone pressed tight against her ear.

"Damn it Taylor, I knew coming here was a bad idea." Taylor, Maria's best friend in the mergers practice of Bradford & Young, had just confirmed the rumor that Maria's chief rival, A.J. Carter, was getting the assignment Maria had hoped for. It was the third time such a plum assignment had gone to someone else.

"You're the best, Maria. That's why Vincent sent you to Rome. Don't worry; there'll be other opportunities."

But Maria wondered. The first time an assignment went to someone else she'd gotten angry and worked even harder. The second time she'd gotten angrier still but then, when the anger died, she'd stopped and examined what was happening. She couldn't work any harder, she reasoned, so she must need to work smarter.

A consultation with some friends and an early mentor confirmed her belief that she needed to prioritize her work and focus on the most important things. But she also took note of a comment her mentor made—the possibility that this was an early sign the firm's leaders didn't think she'd make partner. That gave her pause and, briefly, she considered ditching the big accounting firm for a smaller one, or going home to the family business. But she couldn't imagine Vincent and the other partners really thinking that way. Maria was a committed career woman, everyone knew that, and she just knew she would make partner at one of the biggest specialty accounting firms in the country.

The eternal meeting place of the Spanish Steps was filling with people and heavy with expectation when Maria reached it and began climbing, her ear still glued to her cell phone. The sun had ducked low, behind the banks and *ristorantes* and shops fronting the piazza. Barely aware of where she was going, she climbed the first set of stairs and sat down in an area she'd settled into a number of evenings lately. With a palm pressed over her opposite ear, she strained to hear over the clamor of voices and carts and engines. "Taylor, I'm thirty-seven. I've been at B&Y for fourteen years. I should be up for partner. It's this year or next, or I probably won't make it."

"You'll make it, Maria. So how's the merger coming?"

"We close next week, then I'm out of here. That damn A.J.—she had to have been all over Vincent while I was gone. If only I'd been in Chicago."

"There'll be other assignments, Maria. Maybe you should ask Frank for the IsoTech merger."

Maria fumed some more, and Taylor muttered a few platitudes, then Maria said good-bye and jammed her cell phone toward the top of her purse. But she missed, and it skittered down a couple of the marble steps before coming to rest beside an older gentleman. He glanced over, picked up the phone, then held it out toward her, smiling. She gave him a sheepish look and went to retrieve it. "Sorry," she said. "Thanks." She sat down a few feet away from him and slid the phone into her purse. She realized as she did that her hand was shaking.

She stared at the fountain at the foot of the steps, feel-

ing quivery, a sense of frustration and helplessness drawing her stomach into a tight knot. This was a sign. She
was about to be passed over in favor of A.J. Carter, for
Christ's sake—a woman whose best talents were
schmoozing and opportunism. How could Vincent even
think of giving her the O'Brien merger? He'd virtually
promised it to Maria. Out of sight, out of mind, though,
that's where she'd been, and she'd left A.J. alone to close
in for the kill. Maria should've turned down the Rome
assignment and stayed in Chicago, promoting herself.
She knew better.

But what could she do now? It appeared A.J. had the
assignment. She wanted to call Vincent and ask him why
he'd done it, ask him what was wrong with her, and if
she'd been branded incapable of making partner. But she
knew she couldn't. Nobody liked a whiner. Still, there
had to be a way to get beyond this. She sensed the plug
being pulled on her career.

After fourteen years at the venerable old accounting
firm, she suddenly felt used, spent. She wanted to get up
and run, scream, do something, but she didn't have the
energy even to rise. Her body felt fused to the marble
steps. She stared at Bernini's sculpture of the leaking boat,
its bilge pumps strain against the relentless sea of the
fountain, the sun-baked warmth of its marble seeping
away into the cool of the evening. She closed her eyes
and listened to the sounds about her—greetings, whispered exchanges, loud debates, exclamations of glee. And
rushing water.

The sound of the water made her think of the creek
that hurried past her family's peach orchard each spring.
There, the irrigation pumps carried water to where it was
needed. Here, the pumps pushed it away from the ludicrous improbability of the marble boat.

She opened her eyes to see a young couple embracing beside the fountain, tender, holding, feeling, loving.
Christ, Maria thought, what's happened to me? She
couldn't even remember the last time she'd felt that way

about a man. Her love life had deteriorated into an occasional one- or two-night stand, utilitarian in purpose, no more lasting than the warmth of the noonday sun. No man could tolerate her inattention or survive her mood swings very long. So now she didn't even try to make things last; all of her energy was focused on making partner. There would be time for relationships, time to enjoy the spoils of her success, once she'd made it.

The rattle of a baby carriage drew her attention. She turned to see a young mother wheeling her infant across the piazza. As the woman passed the fountain, Maria noticed a small boy, maybe eight, climbing onto the metal railing encircling it. Seemingly intent on walking atop the rail, the boy managed only a few steps before he slipped and tumbled, flat on this back, into the water. Maria gasped, but the boy popped right up, unharmed, soaking wet. She smiled, then laughed.

The older man near her had started, then half risen, but sat back down as the boy recovered.

"Someone you know?" Maria said, glancing over at him and noting his concern.

"My grandson," he said, through creased old lips. "He is like his father, Franco—always experimenting." The man turned, and his gentle blue eyes found Maria's. "This is the first time I've seen you smile, *signorina*. You should not let things trouble you so. You are very beautiful when you smile."

"Thank you," she said, accepting the compliment she'd found typical of Italian men, especially the older ones. "Are you from Rome?"

"No, no," he said. "We have a vineyard outside the city."

"Really? My family owns a peach orchard in the U.S. In middle Georgia."

"Ah, *signorina*, then you work as I do, with the fruit of the land."

"Actually, I work for an accounting firm. I'm here supporting a big merger team."

"Is it something you can tell me about?"

"It's all very secretive, I'm afraid."

The man nodded. He had a gentle face. Familiar somehow.

"Your English is very good. Do you come into the city often?"

"My other son Gianni does. He handles our finances—the banking, the contracts with the distributors, the merchants. He is with them this afternoon. This weekend, we've all come to Rome, though—to hear Pavarotti."

"Really? Pavarotti is in town? I've always wanted to see him in person. Do you suppose there are any tickets left?"

"I would not think so, *signorina*. His performances, they are usually booked for months in advance."

"That's too bad. I wish I had known earlier." Maria paused. "I should pay more attention to these things." She stared again at the fountain, and at the father who was trying to dry his son off.

"However," the man said, then paused. Maria sensed him looking at her and turned. There was a twinkle in his eye. "My other son, Gianni, he could probably get a ticket through his friend from the university. His friend studied with Luciano, and always has tickets for Gianni. I would be happy to ask him for you." A smile crinkled his weathered complexion.

Maria smiled at his kindness. "Oh, that would be wonderful," she said. "But I don't want to inconvenience you."

"My dear, everyone should hear Luciano at least once. It is the experience of a lifetime. Myself, I have heard him a dozen or more times now, and I never tire of it. I wish for you that you should hear him, too. I will ask Gianni."

"Thank you so much."

The man slid closer. "So why do you not work in your family business? Do you not like the orchards? Your family, do they not need you?"

She held his gaze for a moment. His question startled her, but it made her think. Why had she left Georgia? For fortune? Fame? To prove herself? To become something more than a peach grower? "I wanted more than our small business could offer, I guess."

"Ah, America—it is the land of opportunity. My Gianni wanted to become a professional like yourself—a lawyer. So we sent him away to the university and he joined a big firm here in Rome when he graduated. After a few years, though, he came back to us in the vineyards. We were glad to have him, of course, and his experience helps us to this day. It is funny, is it not, how we sometimes discover that what we love isn't what we wanted?"

Maria smiled at him—at his wisdom born of age and experience. She respected that. "Yes," she said. "It is funny."

"So you, do you love what you have achieved?"

The question cut, and it made her think of Vincent and A.J. and the last fourteen years and she realized that, for the past few minutes, her mind had been in a different place, a peaceful place, among the peach trees and the vineyards and the running water. "I thought I had," she said, then looked away.

"Ah, I must go now," the man said, standing up.

Maria followed his eyes to the fountain. The young boy beside it exclaimed something to his father, then raced away toward a woman carrying packages in both hands. The woman put the packages down as the boy approached and leaned over to hug him. Then she held him at arm's length and glanced toward his father with a look that seemed to say simultaneously, 'what happened?' and 'not again!'

The elderly man reached into his pocket. "Here is my card. We are staying at the St. Regis Grand Hotel. Call me in the morning and I will let you know about the ticket." He excused himself then and left, and Maria realized as she watched him descend the steps that he had left behind a palpable void. Funny. She usually welcomed being alone.

She read the card. Antonio Rosetti and Sons, it said. Winemakers. She looked up and watched them go, the grandfather, the son, the daughter-in-law and the grandson, each with their own gait, each maintaining pace with one another, animated in their conversation. She watched until they disappeared beyond the obelisk in front of the Spanish Embassy and down one of the streets beyond. Then she sat for a long time, plotting how she'd get her career back on track.

She wanted to call Vincent and tell him he was crazy and to go to hell, but aside from the temporary good feeling it'd give her, it would in no way get her back into management's good graces. In the end, she came back to taking the IsoTech merger like Taylor had said, and using it to prove she was better than A.J. IsoTech was up in Milwaukee, not far from Chicago, so she'd be close by to protect her backside. Yeah, that had definite possibilities. If she went back to the office now, she could use the weekend to read up on the account.

She started to rise, but became aware of the sun having set and of darkness falling. Around her, the piazza had filled with people. Couples were pairing off and slipping away to some nearby *ristorante*, others were sitting and talking, still others were touching, kissing. She listened, as she had on other nights, to their whispers, to their exclamations, to the constant stream of water flowing from the pumps in the fountain. And she felt the cool of evening settle on her bare arms and neck.

Finally she rose and turned away from the office, toward the artful steps that joined heaven and earth. They were bathed now in artificial light, as was the obelisk at the top. The Egyptian artifact had belonged to Sallust, a governor of Julius Caesar's, and seemed something of a crown. She climbed to the first landing, then the second, stepping around absorbed lovers and sulking loners. She reached the obelisk and stood for several minutes, peering over the rooftops of Rome, to the Forum, to the Vittorio Emanuele II monument, to the dome of St. Peter's and the Vatican. What was it about this place? It did something to her inside—made her feel empty and alone, despite all the people. She turned toward the Church of *Trinità dei Monti* that stood behind the obelisk. Its twin bell towers reached high into the night sky, maintaining watch over the steps and the city below. Its presence felt comforting.

There were very few people on this level, and movement along the narrow street in front of the church caught her eye. She glanced toward a tall, slim Italian woman in a tailored blue suit, white blouse and spike heels, moving fast, all business, probably on her way home from working late in a nearby office. A young girl darted in front of her at the church steps and was almost trampled, as the woman never broke stride. Maria closed her eyes then, and saw herself on the way home, just like this woman, every evening for the past four months.

Have I become as cold as that? Maria wondered. As focused as that? The question slammed like a loose shutter against the hardened façade of her self-perception. It seemed lately that there was only work for her—in the office, at home, on the weekends—nothing else mattered. She closed her eyes again, and the shuttered window opened and she saw herself there, trapped.

She realized then that she'd lost herself somewhere in her climb up the steps of success, lost what was important, the things she valued. For a few moments earlier her mind had retreated to a place that felt good again, and she liked that. She needed to take more time for herself, for her spirit. For a split second, she again considered telling Vincent to shove it. But that was silly; she had a career. She pushed the feeling aside.

The doorman pushed the big glass doors open for Maria, and she hurried inside, fearing she may be too late. But, as she turned toward the desk, she saw the elder Rosetti. He looked up as she approached.

"Ah, *signorina*, I was leaving the ticket here for you."

"I'm sorry. I had intended to be here sooner. I hope I didn't keep you."

"Not at all. We like to get to the concert hall early." He held out an envelope.

Maria took the envelope and touched his hand. She noticed the form of it—the short, thick fingers with dense patches of graying hair between the joints, the backs dark with the sun, the nails cropped close, the palm and finger pads heavily calloused. A sensation of familiarity flooded over her.

"Thank you so much. How much do I owe you?"

"Please, *signorina*, you owe me nothing. It is our gift to you—to hear Luciano. You can thank my son for getting you the ticket." The old man smiled, and his grizzled hand gestured to someone behind her.

Maria turned to find a man about her age with crystal blue eyes, longish brown hair and sun-baked skin. His suit was practical but well made, his tie expensive. A short scar under his left eye interrupted the strong line of his cheekbones. She felt an immediate warmth toward him. "You must be Gianni," she said, extending her hand. "I want you to know how much I appreciate your kindness."

"It is my pleasure, *signorina*. Especially for someone so far from home—and so beautiful. My father was right—you have an incredible smile." He took her hand, and gently brushed it with his lips.

Maria blushed.

"Your seat is beside mine," he said. "We would be honored if you would accompany us to the concert hall. We will have some wine there, and some cheese, and we can get acquainted before the performance. My father tells me your family has a peach orchard in the United States."

Maria considered his proposition only for a moment.

She was enjoying this new luxury; Chicago seemed irrelevant. "Yes," she said. "We do. And I would be pleased to accompany you."

"Then let us be off," he said, and took her arm gently at the elbow and turned her toward the front door.

As she turned, Maria spotted Gianni's brother, and his wife and son, waiting for them by the door. Family, she thought. That's what these people have that I don't. She decided then that she needed to call her family more, visit more; she'd virtually abandoned them. Her father wasn't able to work the orchards anymore, so things had to be tougher now on her mother and brothers. And she thought then of Rosetti's hands, still strong, still able, but so much like her father's. And she realized that Gianni and his brother were lucky.

"I hear you used to be an attorney," Maria said. "How do you like working now in the family business? "

"It is a joy every day. I will tell you more about it over our glass of wine."

She fell into step then, between Gianni and his father and headed for the exit, feeling right at home.

The Nun's Supper
by Phillip Dibble

Nine o'clock on Good Friday morning found Sister Mary Melena sitting at the bedside of her oldest friend, Sr. Mary Kunigunda. Sr. Kunigunda was in the last stages of heart failure, the Cheyne Stokes breathing becoming slower and deeper until it ceased completely. Now it was over and Sr. Mary Melena found herself the last of her order. She called the nurse, kissed her friend goodbye, then crossed herself. She heaved her bulky body out of the room and left the hospital to return to the small building that served as the convent for the order. Is an order of one really an order?

She sat in her tiny room, only a crucifix decorating the whitewashed walls. A tear rolled down her cheek but her sorrow was only for herself. Feeling abandoned by God, the Christ, and her friends, nothing remained. There were no tasks to be performed, no prayers to be rendered. She thought of her bridegroom, the Christ, dying those many years ago at Golgotha. His final words, "My God, why hast thou forsaken me?" followed by, "It is finished." Yes, it is finished.

Sr. Melena waddled slowly around her cell. Christ celebrated a last supper on the night he was betrayed, why not do the same? She perked up a bit; the thought of a supper with foods of her own choosing could be transcendent. She would go shopping.

She moved slowly into the *Campo di Fiori*, her thighs

wet with sweat as they slid against one another. The heat from her heavy brown habit and veil heightened the effort of her movements. Her feet, bound in heavy stockings and ugly brown sandals, felt like moist boots beneath her elephantine legs. She was hungry. Too long she had denied herself the true pleasures of the table. When she first entered the order at fifteen, she was often caught stealing food from the kitchen or from the meager larders of the other nuns. Punishment from Mother Superior soon stopped this behavior. She confined herself to gluttony at the community table. Always eating, always hungry. Her appetite became a cause for her prayers for forgiveness and for her occasional self-flagellation. Hadn't she lived the past thirty-five years as a good hearted and loyal member of the order? This was true, but what had she done for The Bridegroom? Her self-punishment was for her own sins, all of it was about her, not Him.

The *Campo* market had everything she needed for the meal. She chose fatty sausages, crusty breads, soft runny cheeses, tomatoes bursting with juice, a small bloody bluish-purple beefsteak, and crisp green arugula. Next the fruit, strawberries red and plump, oranges with their green stems. Then came the cake and custard. The only wine she had ever tasted was communion wine, so she chose the only label she knew, a bottle of Chianti.

Sr. Melena lugged her self and her parcels back to the convent and spread them out upon the large kitchen table. She lit the burners of the old gas stove, put a kettle on one of them then returned to her chair looking at her treasures for a long time. She thought of the darkness at Golgatha, the silent dying Christ, and she knew what to do. He had died for her, what could she do for him?

When the answer came to her, she rose again from the table, lurched to the stove and blew out the flames leaving only the gas to hiss away in the closed room.

The Guide

by Carolyn Buchanan

It was four o'clock. Charles Brighton parked the car a thousand miles away from the entrance to the ruins of Pompeii, and walked past all the swarthy hucksters with their cheap plastic trinkets of assorted gods and goddesses, following his wife.

"Miranda. Sweetheart. It's late. We can come back in a couple of days, on our way to Sorrento. Everyone's leaving, for chrissakes; there aren't any guided tours this late."

"Don't be obtuse, Charles. These people are poor. They need money. We'll find someone to take us through."

"*Scusi, signore.*" Miranda, aflame in an orange Fila jogging outfit, elbowed her way in front of a gaggle of somber-suited Japanese tourists to the *biglietteria*. The woman in the booth did not even bother to hide her disgust as Miranda stood on tiptoe to shout at her through the round opening in the glass. "*A che ora...* do you close? *Chiude. Chiude!*"

Charles winced. Miranda had learned just enough Italian to irritate the hell out of him.

Miranda turned to Charles and said, *sotto voce*, "God, these people!"

Charles had to agree with her there. You'd think these Italians weren't grateful for all the money Americans dropped over here. Miranda's spending alone had probably paid the porter's entire yearly salary at the hotel.

She tipped the waiters too damn much, too. And of course they all sucked up to her. They knew a gold mine when they saw one.

"*Quattro e trenta.* Four-thirty," snapped the woman at the ticket booth. "No time *ora.*" She waved her hand. "Too late."

Charles stepped up beside Miranda, ignoring the ching-chong outcries of the Japanese behind him.

"My wife wants to see the ruins," he sighed. "Two tickets." He reached into the secret anti-theft pocket sewn inside his silk jacket, and pulled out a cache of Euros held together with an18-karat money clip. Stuffing two twenties into the hole—twice as much as it cost—he carefully replaced the plug of money, planted his feet and crossed his arms, resting them on his richly-fed belly.

When the woman slid two tickets under the opening at the bottom of the glass, Miranda snatched them up, and they started for Pompeii.

Charles followed behind Miranda, huffing up the narrow street, cobbled with black volcanic rock to two side-by-side tunnels, arching like great stone eyebrows above the gates to the dead Etruscan city. There was a continuous stream of people exiting out the arch to his left. Sensible people, going home. Charles and Miranda entered the one on the right.

As they emerged from the underpass and stepped into the ancient city, Charles was struck by the expanse of columns and walls of brittle, gray stone. Crumbing and in pieces now, they stood defiantly, skeletons of another world. Miranda picked her way between the rocks.

"God, I'm ruining my heels on these damn things," she said as she stumbled at his side.

Charles caught her elbow to steady her. She was as surprised as he at the gesture.

"Are you all right?" she asked after a pause.

He let go of her arm, embarrassed. "As all right as I can be, dragging my ass around in ruins when I'm starving."

She fixed him with a piercing look. "I thought you were trying to lose weight. Working out during your lunch hour. Shopping for a sports car—growing your hair longer in the back. At your age." Miranda flipped the hair at the nape of his neck. He flicked her fingers away, scowling, and she laughed—a brittle sound that the wind caught and carried.

"At least I'm *trying* to keep in shape." His father had taught him that the best defense was a good offense. "You look like a blob of orange Jell-O in that damn get up."

"You'll pay for that," she said, and walked a few yards away. Charles hesitated before following her to an area partially enclosed by pocked stone walls. The base of a building dominated the center of the square. Remnants of a row of Ionic columns, like fluted tree stumps, lined the four sides. There were wide steps in the front.

They minced across the cobblestones to the site.

"Wonder what this thing was?" Miranda said, yawning.

"The Temple of Apollo," replied a voice at Charles's shoulder.

He started. A man, dressed in a rumpled black suit and open-collar shirt stood beside him.

"Who in the hell are you?" popped out of Charles. After a beat, he added, "You scared the shit out of me." The man didn't answer.

Charles turned to his wife. "He doesn't speak English—how do you say 'shit' in Italian?"

"Oh, *si. Parla Inglese.* I am Egnatius Severus. I give you a tour, yes?"

"Wonderful." Miranda broke in. She cut her eyes over to Charles. "I told you they would make an exception for money."

"For money? No. It is my pleasure to show you Pompeii."

"How charming." Miranda edged closer to her husband. "Charles, don't you find the Italians charming?"

"I'll bet even money," Charles muttered, "that charm has a price tag attached."

Egnatius led them into the temple. "You mark—the god, Apollo," he said, pointing to a bronze statue still guarding the temple. "The people worshipped him. They believed he would protect them."

"Well, he certainly didn't protect them from that volcano eruption, did he?" Miranda said.

"Ah, the *signora* is so correct. A statue is only the metal, you see? Protection from evil comes from the heart." Egnatius looked deeply into Charles' eyes and held them a shade too long for comfort. Was the man drunk? Charles sniffed discreetly. He didn't smell whiskey on the Italian's breath, but you never knew. The guide turned and contemplated the temple sadly, it seemed to Charles. Egnatius walked over to the god, captured in mid-stride, and laid his hands on the black feet. "He reaches for gold, but holds only the air." He rapped gently on the leg of the giant. Charles heard the hollow echo.

He thought about the nights he'd told Miranda he was working late; the times he'd slipped into Susan's bed. Charles told himself it wasn't his fault; Miranda was cold and demanding, and what was a man to do? He stole a glance at Miranda, listening eagerly to this guide whom Charles suddenly disliked. As he crossed over to Egnatius, he dug into his pocket for a ten Euro.

"Well, uh, Egnostic, that is really interesting about Apollo. You people are really into these gods and things, even now." He handed Egnatius the crisp paper bill. "Thanks, but we really should be getting along. I imagine the gates will close soon."

Egnatius waved away the money, shook his head and smiled. "There are no gates closed to me. I will show you quickly some of the homes, with the beautiful gardens and murals, yes?" He smiled at Miranda.

"Oooh, yes, that would be lovely. And don't they have some of—you know—the people? I mean, the bodies of some of the poor people who died here?" Miranda was getting worked up. Houses were one thing; corpses were another.

"For God's sake, Miranda. It's getting dark. Let the man go home to his family."

"I have no home now. So you see, it is no problem." Egnatius took Miranda's elbow in his left hand, and pressed Charles gently on the shoulder with his right. "There is a very fine house here. I know it well. It will take just a moment, and then I will show you something very *di grande effetto*. Impressive. It will change you, yes?" Before Charles could protest, the Italian turned and walked briskly down the sandy side of the cobbled main street, with Miranda at his heels.

Egnatius led them down one of the side streets, and into the wide entry of a private residence. Even in its state of decay, it was spectacular. Two of the four Corinthian columns of the front portico still stood like weary sentinels. The three of them passed into what was once the foyer.

"Very fine. *Cara*—expensive. Look at the marble still on the floors, the walls." Egnatius called their attention to a round marble base in the center of the hall. "Here was *bella fontana*. Beautiful fountain, with Neptune in the center, and the dolphins around."

"You appreciate fine things, do you?" Miranda asked.

"*Si, signora*. But there are many kinds of riches." Egnatius's fingers delicately traced the outlines of the faded mural painted centuries ago on the walls of the entryway.

Miranda leaned toward Charles and murmured, "Looks like he could use more riches of the monetary kind, if he's working as a tour guide."

Instantly it seemed, Egnatius was at her side.

"We are all guides for someone, no? If we are not helpful in this life, what is to become of us in the next?" The man almost whispered this. Miranda felt his breath on her ear, bristling the hairs on her neck.

"Well," she sputtered, "you certainly do seem to know a lot. I mean, about this house. Whose was it, anyway?" It amused Charles to see her taken aback. "It was the home of a very wealthy man, *signora.* He prized his things, his pleasures, above all else."

Their guide then directed them into the large dining room. A mural, painted in yellow ochres, burnt siennas and aquamarines was still lovely despite the patches broken off the stucco. Like Pompeii itself, it was a jigsaw puzzle with pieces missing. The floor, however, was amazingly intact. An intricate mosaic pattern, it featured a large center medallion in contrasting tiles.

"Now *this* is a house." Miranda pouted at Charles. "This man knew how to take care of his wife."

"Ah, the *signora* loves the beautiful things, yes? But the beauty of these things does not last. Love is wasted on such as this, you agree?"

Miranda moved away from the tour guide, on the pretense of studying the remains of an elaborately carved frieze above the doorway. She remembered the hurt look in Charles's eyes last month when, across the table at a dinner party, she'd accused him of being a tightwad. Did she really need to re-design the master bath? Well yes, she did. She simply had to have her own private bath. After all, Charles was such a slob. Miranda watched Charles wander through the relics of what had once been an important home. He looked so unhappy that for a second, she wanted to apologize. But then she remembered his crack about her weight. Miranda crossed her arms over her heavy breasts. She was ready to get out of this place.

"This really is something," Miranda said, "But my husband is right...we really must leave now. You've been so kind. Pay the nice Italian, Charles. I know you must be getting hungry."

Charles gave Miranda a grateful look, and dug out the crumpled bill, offering it again to the guide. Once again, he politely refused.

"Five minutes more, *signora*. We go to see one of the lost people of Pompeii." Egnatius put his right hand gently on Miranda's back, and extended his left hand, showing the way. Charles pulled up the cuff of his sweater and looked elaborately at his watch. Miranda glanced back at him, her eyebrows raised, but she kept walking. In a matter of moments, they were standing in an ancient room. In the center, in a transparent coffin, was the mummy of a lone Pompeian man. Miranda fished around in her purse for her camera. "I want to get a picture of this. Charles, stand by the case." Charles heard the high-pitched whine of the Leica as she turned it on.

Charles stared into Egnatius's eyes for a moment. "I don't know, Miranda. Maybe it's not... right."

Miranda lowered the camera. "Why? They died so quickly; they didn't know what hit them anyway. Right?" She turned to Egnatius.

"*Signora*, regard." Egnatius swept his hand along the length of the display case. "What do you see?"

Miranda peered into the box. The man's legs were bent, his arms crossed tightly against his chest. His mouth was twisted in a grimace, baring his teeth.

"Hmmm. Well, I suppose he *does* look like he's in agony."

"Yes. Forever agony. Do you still choose to take your photograph?"

Miranda hesitated.

Charles shifted impatiently. "Come on, Miranda. Who gives a damn about some poor bastard who's been dead a thousand years? Let's go." He sighed, and pulled a cigar out of a leather case in his breast pocket.

Miranda shot him a hateful look. "This is a non-smoking area."

"What am I gonna do? Burn the place down...again?" Charles laughed at his own joke, bit the end off the Havana and spit it into the rubble.

"Very funny. Stand over there, on that side of the

mummy." She turned to the guide, watching the scene somberly. "What did you say your name was, again?"

"Egnatius. Egnatius Severus."

"Egnatius, would you be a darling and take our picture with this thing?"

The guide frowned. "But *signora,* I thought—"

"For God's sake, man, get on with it," Charles cried.

"As you wish," Egnatius said quietly.

Charles chewed on his cigar and watched as the Italian held the camera up to his pale face.

Pop! The flash irritated Charles. His hands flew up to shield his eyes.

"Great. You've got your photo. Now can we please get the hell out of here?"

Pop! Another flash. "Enough!" cried Charles. "Idiot," he grumbled.

Pop, pop! Blue-white light exploded into yellow spots that faded to black, blinding his vision. Pop, pop, pop!

Charles glanced to his side. The constant blips of laser bright light lent a surreal, black-light effect to the now dark surroundings. He saw Miranda sink to her knees in a kind of jerky, slow motion. He stared as she looked up at him in astonishment, her mouth opening and closing without sound, like a fish out of water, gasping for air. With great effort, she pointed to the brass plaque on the front of the mummy's case. Charles squinted. In the intermittent illumination of the flashbulb he read the name: SEVERUS.

At four o'clock the next day, as the weak winter sun began to fade on the ruins of Pompeii, the last group of tourists stood gawking. Cameras whirred and flash bulbs popped as the curious onlookers snapped their souvenir photographs of the corpses on display in the ancient room. In the center, the withered body of a Pompeian man lay in his glass coffin, captured forever in his last agony. Flanking him on either side, two additional mummies were displayed, each in its own crystal case: a woman crouched in one, her face hidden by her hands; in the other a man, crab-like, was frozen in a desperate crawl.

"Bummer," complained a teen-ager, slouched over one of the coffins. "There's only three of them?"

A man, dressed in a rumpled black suit stepped out of the shadows.

"Ah, there will be more," he said sadly, shaking his head. "There will be many more."

The Mistress' Sapphire
by Barbara de Normandie

Alessia never deviated from her monthly pampering regime at the Tuscan spa, but a wife must break the mold sometimes. She scratched softly behind Giuseppe's ear as her private jet descended into Rome for an unannounced visit with her husband, Bruno Cheradini. Bruno would be furious with her for interrupting his business trip, but she needed a Rome-fix to celebrate Giuseppe's brilliant first place performance at The International Dog Show in Milan.

Only the entry light greeted her as she unlocked the door and directed the driver to deposit her seven bags into her dressing room. Giuseppe lay snuggled within her embrace until they stood alone in the cavernous living room. Setting the dog on the divan, she poured herself a glass of wine and stood by the window admiring the panoramic view of the *Citta Del Vaticano* and *Castel Sant'Angela*.

"Tonight, Giuseppe," she said as she sat down beside her dog, " we will celebrate your victory. Papa will take us to the best restaurant in Rome and you shall drink the best champagne from a fine crystal goblet. And, as a special treat, you shall select which outfit I shall wear tonight."

Giuseppe bounded onto her lap and released a barrage of kisses all over her face. Alessia waited until Giuseppe had settled down again, then pulled a brush out of her purse and began grooming the dog with loving attention. She purred with delight at the pleasure Giuseppe derived from this simple exercise.

Their snuggle was interrupted when Bruno stomped through the front foyer to fulfill his role brilliantly in their play of life. "What are you doing here? I gave you a strict instructions to meet me in Venice in three days. Can't I even conduct business without you hovering around with that ridiculous lap dog?"

Alessia chose to ignore him, and continued grooming Giuseppe and sipping her wine. Bruno continued his tirade for a moment more and then silence descended upon the room. Apparently, Bruno had decided to break the mold, too.

He placed his briefcase and a parcel wrapped in gold paper on the marble coffee table. She dutifully presented both china-white cheeks to be kissed. The contrast in their skin tones always amused her, her porcelain skin seemed polished against his olive tones.

"Please forgive me for my abrupt entrance, my dear. It's been a difficult day and I have a very intense..." He paused for a moment and then continued, "yes, intense meeting this evening and I still have some work to do."

Alessia delicately placed the brush back into her purse and smiled innocently at Bruno. She brushed a strand of hair from her face and formed her award-winning pout. "But, Bruno, we have such important news and I know my mother would be most distressed to learn that you weren't able to share in Giuseppe's celebration. He took first place at the dog show."

Bruno turned his back to her, but not fast enough to hide his scowl. Alessia's mother owned the company Bruno worked for and The International Dog Show was her pet project. While Alessia challenged Bruno to defy the family, she watched Giuseppe jump off the sofa and slip away with the beautifully wrapped parcel in the delicate golden filagree paper.

Bruno took a deep breath. "I know how much this

show means to you and your mother, but it is imperative that I attend this meeting tonight. Might I suggest that I clear my calendar for tomorrow afternoon and we'll make it a grand celebration complete with a full pet party and some of Giuseppe's four-legged friends? I might even have a surprise or two for you."

She was disappointed, but pet parties were the rage in the U.S. She could start a whole new trend across Rome. And, she loved surprises. She reluctantly agreed to a delayed celebration and made arrangements to meet friends at a posh new wine bar in *Piazza Barberini.*

Bruno had gone to his bedroom to change and Alessia was sorting through her luggage in her own room when she heard the sound of breaking glass, gagging and yelps of pain. She dropped the designer dress on the tile mosaic floor and raced to the kitchen.

There she found Bruno holding Giuseppe on the counter top while attempting to disgorge something from the dog's tiny mouth with his large forefinger. Judging from the blood on Bruno's hand, the dog was winning the battle.

He released the dog and retreated to the sink explaining that he broke a glass. "I think Giuseppe might have eaten a shard. I could be mistaken, but it seems we should take the dog to a veterinarian."

"And, where to you plan to find a vet at this time of night?" She was livid. "How could you be so clumsy and then be irresponsible enough to let Giuseppe even come into the kitchen?" She wanted to jab a shard or two down Bruno's throat.

Bruno's olive complexion glistened with sweat and Alessia actually started to feel sorry for her husband. He seemed genuinely concerned about Giuseppe.

"Since I caused this most unfortunate situation, the least I could do is take Giuseppe to Sebastiani just to make sure everything's okay. He's kind of a recluse, so it's best if I go alone. But, I promise to call as soon as the vet gives me a report." Bruno didn't wait for Alessia's approval and left with Giuseppe tucked under one arm and his overcoat under the other.

Alessia planned to leave the broken glass for the maid when a shimmer under the cabinet caught her eye. She bent down to retrieve the remains of the golden filagree wrapping paper. Tiny amounts of chocolate and raspberry smeared on her fingers as she grabbed the paper. She didn't find glass shards anywhere except in the sink.

Then the strangest thought crossed her mind. What if the blood had actually been raspberry sauce? Raspberry sauce inside a chocolate delight wrapped in golden filagree paper consumed by Giuseppe. An investigation of the counter top and kitchen sink confirmed her suspicions and it puzzled Alessia enough that she pulled on her coat hoping to find Bruno and her dog at the only vet Bruno knew in Rome.

Alessia was admitted to the home of Sebastiani Ladogana by a surly butler with no chin and even less grace. She waited in the foyer for an eternity before being admitted to a office at the bottom of spiral staircase two stories below ground. Giuseppe rested quietly on the operating table obviously sedated with his stomach shaved and stitches visible.

Sebastiani greeted her in the customary way with a kiss on each cheek, but refused to make eye contact. Bruno started babbling about having to react quickly and not being able to phone her in a more timely manner. Alessia stood stunned at the sight before her.

Her beloved pet was damaged. Cut and sewn up like a common rag doll. She could never show Giuseppe to the world again with such disfiguration. Where would she find another such perfect animal again? Her fury seethed forth.

"You butcher, what have you done to my Giuseppe? I'll have your license, your home and your first born for this barbarous act of carving my innocent baby!"

Then she saw the shiny object on the tray with the operating instruments. The small sculptured item still had chocolate and gold paper clinging to the smooth surfaces, but she knew what it was. The iridescent cerulean glow reflected the bright operating room lights. Alessia Cheradini knew her stones and this was the biggest sapphire ring she'd ever seen.

Her gaze rotated mechanically toward Bruno, and followed his gaze to his open briefcase. A photo of him and a woman half Alessia's age wearing sapphire earrings lay on top of a card. Bruno didn't say a word, but the look of guilt and humiliation explained everything.

This jeweled gift had not been meant for her. Silently, she cradled her dog in her arms and left Dr. Ladogana's home and eventually Rome for the last time. With her mother's help, Bruno would pay dearly and she'd end up with the ring and the matching set of earrings, too!

One Thorn Among Many

by Eldon Thompson

Pagus leaned into his work, moving the rake efficiently among the hedgerows of his master's private garden. It was light toil, really. In some ways, he rather enjoyed it. The garden was beautiful to be sure, a flowering atrium teeming with sweet scents and vibrant colors. More importantly, it was a place of quiet, the one location to which he could escape to be alone with his thoughts. Sometimes, while laboring among the plants and shade trees, he was able to forget almost completely the truth of his place in the world. Despite the aches and pains and occasional blister, it was perhaps the most enjoyable of his duties.

He bent to pick up a stone. As he came up, another bounced at his feet, as though falling from an overhead tree. He looked up, scanning the foliage. Sure enough, there was Fabius, crouched on a rooftop that lay beyond the encircling wrought iron fence, his ruddy face creased with a stupid grin. Pagus watched as the son of Master Cornelius reached into a leather pouch, pulled forth a stone, and flung it right at him. It was a good throw. Pagus actually had to dodge in order to avoid a nasty thump to the skull.

Biting back his anger, Pagus turned to collect the stones. He could hear Fabius' laughter as he worked, and did his best to ignore the continuing barrage, other than to note where each missile had landed so that he could retrieve it. He wondered briefly how severe might be the punishment should he decide to throw one or more of them right back. It might well be a price worth paying. Nevertheless, it was a passing thought. He had no wish to embarrass himself or his master, who would suffer insults from the community for having selected such a rebellious youth as his chief servant. Nor did he wish to give Fabius the satisfaction of a reaction of any sort. In the end, it was best for all to just keep silent.

"Fabius," a voice rang out severely.

From where he knelt, Pagus glanced up to see Cornelius Jucundus, Duumvir of Pompeii, cutting a path through the inner courtyard. The master's eyes were fixed upon his son's rooftop position. Through the corner of his eye, Pagus watched as Fabius withered beneath his father's stern gaze, abandoning his assault and slinking from view. When he had gone, Master Cornelius produced a key and stepped through the gate that marked the entrance to his garden, approaching Pagus' location.

Pagus rose to his feet and bowed. "I am sorry to have offended him, Master."

Cornelius shook his head. "It would seem my son is offended with life these days. We can only hope that he will grow out of it."

Pagus bowed again.

"May I?" Cornelius asked.

Pagus stepped out of the way, allowing his master to walk past until he had reached an array of rose bushes that sprouted in the exact center of the garden. One rose in particular stood tall and proud among the others, its stem stripped of thorns save one. Cornelius did not hesitate, but reached up and pressed his thumb squarely upon the tip of the thorn, wincing only slightly as he drew blood. He then tipped his head back and drew a deep breath, closing his eyes against a stream of sunlight. At last, he turned and walked back toward the garden entrance, pausing to place a hand upon Pagus' shoulder as he went.

"Life grants us another day," the older man said.

Pagus nodded, then faithfully repeated his half of the ritualistic exchange. "Let us do with it as we may."

Cornelius patted the younger man on the shoulder, leaving him to his work.

Pagus lay in his private quarters that night, thinking as he often did of who he was and who he might one day be. He had just about fallen asleep when the attack woke him. Though he could not remember any sensory triggers, he must have felt it coming, for he bolted upright in bed an instant before it happened, his eyes snapping open to stare into moonlit darkness. As soon as he did so, the attacker was there, pressing a dagger against his throat. Pagus held his breath as a sneering face thrust itself into view.

Fabius.

Pagus blinked several times to be sure of what was happening. He started to speak, but the other signaled silence. A moment later, Fabius whispered, "We've been summoned."

Pagus swallowed hard and nodded, doing what he could to disguise his fear. He must have failed, because Fabius' smirk only widened as he pulled Pagus to his feet.

Moments later, they had worked their way outside the house and into the streets. A gusting wind blew down the roads and alleys, chilling Pagus' skin. Pagus shivered, but said not a word. He glanced at Fabius, who prodded him forward with the dagger, saying nothing about where they were going, or why.

At the end of the block, Fabius shoved him into an alley. There, Pagus came face-to-face with a young man, a beggar by the looks of him. After a moment, however, Pagus was surprised to realize that he recognized the lad.

"Lucretius," Pagus whispered in stunned greeting.

Lucretius hissed at him to be silent, then motioned both Pagus and Fabius into the deep shadows. There, he took a moment to look Pagus up and down, as though sizing him up for some task. "Congratulations, Pagus," he said finally. "You are about to win your freedom."

Pagus stared at the young man, dumbfounded. Lucretius was well known to him, a chief servant with whom he had often met. The boy's master was none other than Sallust Severus, a close friend of Master Cornelius and a prominent citizen in his own right.

Lucretius cast about furtively, then produced a folded square of leather. He opened it up to reveal what appeared to be an oily frog skin.

"Poison," he explained. "A venom which, when it reaches the blood stream, can fell a horse within minutes."

Pagus studied the item, then looked up at Lucretius, confusion mirrored in his eyes.

"My master wishes to be elected Duumvir next month. He would not care to lose out to yours a second time."

Pagus gaped wordlessly. He glanced at Fabius. "You're going to poison your father?"

Fabius snickered. "No, Pagus. You are."

Pagus groped for a response that would not come, his lips forming any number of unspoken words. "I...I have no cause," he stammered at last.

"No cause?" Fabius laughed quietly. "You are a slave, Pagus."

"You are being given an opportunity," Lucretius agreed, pulling forth a scroll and extending it to the other. "Do this one thing, and my master is prepared to secure your freedom."

Pagus accepted the scroll, and after a moment's hesitation, read its inscription. A sudden twinge tickled his spine. The writ was a proclamation of freedom, signed already by Sallust Severus, Duumvir of Pompeii. Help the man to assume the position, and he would be free.

Pagus glanced quickly between the two conspirators,

horror and disbelief crowding for dominance of his features. "Why me?"

Again, Fabius laughed, this time, without any trace of mirth. "You are the only one, other than Father, with access to his private garden. Who else?"

"I am to poison the man in his own house?"

"The venom must enter the bloodstream," Fabius said, reiterating Lucretius' description. He stared at Pagus meaningfully.

Pagus shook his head, as if by doing so he might clear away this curious nightmare. What had Master Cornelius ever done that he should help to take the man's life? "I cannot do this," he said at last.

"Be smart," Lucretius urged him. "Your master is not long for this earth. Do not suffer for some misguided loyalty. Take this opportunity to profit from his demise."

Pagus turned back to Fabius. He could deduce easily enough the son's stake in this affair. With Cornelius gone, Fabius would become master of House Jucundus.

"Refuse this act," Fabius said, "and I will see you branded a thief and driven into the streets, so that another may take your place in my father's garden."

Lucretius took back the scroll and plucked forth a bag of coins, which he pressed into Pagus' hand. "This is but a first payment," he promised. "You shall be paid thrice over when the deed is done."

Pagus stared wide-eyed into the open bag, feeling its weight bearing down upon him. He looked slowly from one face to the other, still unable to believe this was happening. He had heard of such murderous intrigue, certainly. But to be drawn into such a plot, here and now...

He glanced from one face to the next. He could not trust either of these men; that much was obvious. But considering the choices... He stared down at the bag of gold, more wealth than he could spend in a lifetime. He thought of all the good he might do with it. He thought of the words of his own master, who had often shared with him philosophies concerning the cycle of life. Death is necessary, Cornelius would claim without a hint of regret. The old must die that the young may take their place. A more natural progression did not exist.

A cloud passed overhead, dimming the light of the moon. A nightbird offered up a shrill cry. Pagus wondered suddenly whether one of his children would one day be crouched in an alley, plotting his own unnatural demise.

"Give me the poison," he said.

A blustery wind swirled in the garden that day, shaking boughs, stirring leaves, and freezing Pagus to the bone. The events of the previous night were a blur. Only when he had awakened that morning to find the bag of gold and leather-wrapped poison skin did he believe that the strange encounter with Fabius, son of Cornelius, and Lucretius, servant of Sallust, had actually taken place. The very idea of what they had asked of him was absurd. But what was he to do? Run to his master with the story? With the evidence in hand, he might just convince the old man of the truth. But to what end? If Fabius and Sallust were determined to see Cornelius dead, what would stop them? Should this attempt fail, another would be undertaken. Even if the two conspirators were rooted out and convicted for their crimes, how long would it be before another followed their lead?

The questions were maddening, a vicious circle of logic and illogic that had made Pagus sick to his stomach. He had gone about his chores that morning without an answer in sight. Although he wanted to deny it, there was a certain amount of temptation that he could not quite overcome. All of a sudden, his dreams were not just fantasies, but possibilities. In any case, this affair was not his decision. He was but a tool, being used as a carpenter might a hammer. If a murderer was caught in the act, which was destroyed, the knife, or the wielder?

He was still pondering these questions as he went into the master's garden that day. He pondered them as he smeared the venomous frog skin onto the master's rose thorn. Enough for one prick, Lucretius had said, and one prick only. But one prick was all it would take. A fitting end, really. For Master Cornelius had explained to Pagus the philosophy behind his strange ritual as the need to remind himself each day that if he could still feel pain, then he was still alive. Only on this day, the scale by which he measured his life would tip in the other direction.

Pagus thought of this as his master approached, stepping through the iron gate. He reminded himself that it was his master's choice, his master's ritual. He was merely a servant, someone who did what he was told. That was his place in the world.

"Good day, Pagus," Cornelius greeted. The old man looked down at him with that kind and knowing expression, seeing right through him, and continued past.

Pagus began to tremble. What had he done? He remembered suddenly another of Cornelius' philosophies, that it was not the treasures accumulated during one's life that mattered, but the manner in which they were claimed. In an instant, the truth was revealed, the arguments and excuses that had covered it skittering away like dry leaves. Pagus knew in that moment that he had been deceived by his own aspirations. He knew in that moment that he had been blinded by the selfish need to improve his station in life. And he knew in that moment that he would sooner perish without achievement or the comforts it might bring than to steal from another that which he had not earned for himself.

Casting aside all other thoughts, Pagus dropped his rake and rushed after his master. He caught the man in two easy strides, then lunged past. Without slowing, he reached the rose bush and pressed his thumb deep onto its lone thorn. One prick, and one prick only. But one prick was all it would take.

He shuddered, feeling a warmth course through his

veins, feeling all doubt and fear drain from him in an instant.

"Pagus?"

The slave turned slowly toward his master, his eyes upon the ground. "I have failed you, Master." He looked up. "Life grants you another day."

Cornelius said nothing for a moment, then smiled sadly. He stepped to one side, sweeping his arm out wide. Through the entrance to the garden, Pagus watched as Fabius was drawn into the courtyard by a pair of guards, thrashing against their hold.

"Unhand me!" Fabius screamed. He stopped when he saw his father. "It was Pagus!" he cried. "He threatened me to keep silent! I wanted to warn you, but he..."

His tirade tapered off as he caught sight of Lucretius stepping free of an alcove, followed by the boy's master, Sallust Severus. The elder man nodded to Cornelius.

Cornelius returned the greeting, then turned his back to his son. He stepped forward and reached out instead to his chief servant. Pagus made no move as the other slipped free the wide leather belt encircling his waist, that which carried the brand of the family Jucundus, the symbol of Pagus' slavery.

"You have proven your loyalty, young Pagus," the older man proclaimed softly. "You are free."

Pagus blinked in confusion.

"There is no poison," Cornelius explained. "The council asked that I nominate a new *aedile*, a member of my household. It was assumed I would select my son, but I was uncertain of his worthiness." He paused. A heavy sigh rattled from his chest as he glanced back at a sullen Fabius. "The council agreed to let me test it—and yours—before a decision was made."

Pagus shook his head, aghast, humiliated, ashamed. "Master, I thought to profit at your expense."

Cornelius offered a compassionate smile. "Had you not been tempted, it would not have been a sacrifice."

"Master, I—"

"Life grants us another day," the older man said.

The young servant studied his master. In the court-yard beyond, Lucretius nodded encouragingly.

Pagus swallowed his pride, swallowed his shame. "Let us do with it as we may."

The Invisible Necklace

by Adrea Mach

April First, Day of Fools, and the day Cara had set to end her life, was only one day away. How had it come to this?

It is said that fools are seekers in disguise, prone to rush in where angels fear to tread. Both descriptions fit Cara to a tee.

Brought up in the American Midwest, she had long sought something better than her wrong-side-of-the-tracks background and had battled the odds to achieve it, ending up geographically far from her jettisoned past, living and working in Europe. In the heyday of her youth, men—and her stepfather in particular—had found her Nordic attractiveness irresistible. But she had finally escaped his sexual abuse too and, after a brief marriage, now lived on her own in Switzerland.

Still, beneath the persona of self-sufficiency, Cara was in crisis. Things had reached rock-bottom over the past winter and Cara, who always finished what she started, had issued herself an ultimatum: *Either turn it around by April—or leave it altogether.* By 'it,' she meant her ill-lived life.

The last commitment on her calendar was one made earlier to spend Easter in Rome. That is how she found herself now as a reluctant pilgrim in the Eternal City, standing before the large, imposing gate that guarded the Order of St. Joseph of the Apparition. An appropriate name, as she was soon to learn.

She pressed the remote control bell inside the grounds of the *casa per feria,* the convent guesthouse where she would be staying. Nothing happened. Then the tall, forest-green doors began to slide open slowly without a sound, as if guided by an invisible hand. As they did so, the sanctuary within revealed itself: lush, well-tended gardens with lilies, roses and rhododendrons beneath a canopy of umbrella pines and palm trees. Cara walked toward the four-story guesthouse, drawing in her breath as she saw the vista of Rome unfolding before her, the Vatican walls and the enormous dome of St. Peter's rising in the afternoon haze like a mirage.

"So this is Annetta's secret paradise," Cara mused, recalling that day of their auspicious meeting just a little over three months ago.

"In the company of angels," began the brochure. "Of course there are amazing sights to be seen in Rome—the Trevi Fountain, the Colosseum, the Egyptian obelisks, the city walls, St. Peter's Square, the Sistine Chapel, the Vatican to name but a few—but that's only part of the story. To get the most out of what can be a spiritually uplifting, even life-changing, visit to Rome, you have to stay at the right place, be with the right people."

Annetta, who had given her the flyer, had come out of nowhere, as spirits are wont to do. She seemed just an ordinary person, an attractive, widowed Englishwoman encountered on the almost empty paddle-wheel steamer that carried them both on that cruise of Lake Geneva just before Christmas. Cara had found herself striking up a conversation with this complete stranger who said she was a seeker, traveling widely and often on her own.

Cara said, "I'm going to Rome in spring to work on a book. I'm looking for a special place, off the beaten tourist track, for inspiration to write." She didn't mention the demons stalking her. But Annetta seemed to sense it and looked at her intently as if scanning another dimension.

Then, as if in response to what she'd seen, her face lit up, and she said, "Oh, I know just the place for you. The *casa per feria* guesthouse run by the sisters of St. Joseph. The perfect place. A *safe* space," she added, answering the unasked question.

Later, as they parted on the quay in Geneva, Annetta drew her aside and said, "Oh, one more thing. To vanquish your dark demons, you must search and find the invisible necklace that holds the secret of your soul. Here's the name of someone in Rome who can help you."

On the slip of paper was the name *Amyra*, nothing more. How had Annetta known? What was this about a magic necklace? And where would she find an "Amyra" in all of Rome? But when Cara looked up to ask, Annetta had disappeared into the December dusk.

Now, three months later as Easter approached, Cara found herself in Rome in the company of the brochure's very own "angels".

"Good afternoon, *buon giorno, buenas dias, bongu,*" the diminutive 76-year old Sister Angelica welcomed her in English, Italian, Spanish, and finally in her native Maltese. And, once again, without any information having been exchanged, she said, "You will need a special space in which to write. I have given you the room our superiors use when they come from France because, if the Lord is speaking to you, it is a blessing and you must listen."

Surprised and embarrassed, Cara moved into her room with a view over Rome and the Vatican walls. From the rooftop terrace, where she went that evening to see the lights of the city, she felt she could almost reach out and touch the illuminated dome of St. Peter's.

The next day was Palm Sunday and Anna-Krystyna, a Polish-American who was also staying at the guesthouse and had spontaneously befriended her, gave her a ticket to attend the outdoor service in St Peter's

Square. Arriving by way of the *Via della Concillazione*, she was overwhelmed by the living, moving mosaic: the procession of swaying green palm branches contrasting with the cardinal's crimson regalia, and the multi-hued costumes of sixty thousand people converging from the far corners of the world.

A cold March wind blustered through the colonnades as the frail Pontiff appeared in his immaculate white and scarlet. Pensive, bowed under the weight of his eighty-two years, he squinted against the brilliant sunshine, valiantly trying to suppress the tremor in his hands by clutching his sceptre, struggling through his homily in a kaleidoscope of languages, interspersed with "Glorias" and "O Dio mio's" sung by the Sistine Chapel choir.

"Is this the last Easter?" Cara asked herself, her heart going out to him for his fortitude and tenacity in the face of physical deterioration. "His time is running out. So is mine."

Nevertheless, the next day Cara took a taxi to the *Campo di Fiori* to absorb the sights and sounds of the Roman marketplace full of flowers, fruits and vegetables, vendors, shoppers and tourists. Out of the milling crowd, a gypsy emerged, approached her and said, "I am Amyra. I have a message for you." Cara was taken aback. How was this possible? Was she being followed?

"No, don't worry," Amyra said, "no one will hurt you—except *forse* (maybe) yourself. Now show me your hand—and I will show you something, too."

Before she could think better of it, Cara extended her hand, palm upwards. The gypsy took it in her brown, gnarled fingers, bending her head down to scrutinize the maze of fine lines crisscrossing Cara's smooth, white skin. After several minutes, Amyra looked up and, with her amber eyes, gazed straight into Cara's cobalt blue ones.

"Ah, Cara *mia*, you look so different but inside you are like us, the *Roma* people, wandering in exile, far from your true home. You are living borrowed lives, warming yourself at others' hearth fires. You must seek until you find your own. This will help you," she said, pulling something from an unseen pocket in her dark, tattered cloak. "What do you see?"

"Why...a necklace!" Cara answered. It was lovely, glowing in the late afternoon sun, its many multi-colored strands interwoven with one another.

"*Bene*. Not everyone sees it. After all, the necklace is invisible to almost all but those to whom it belongs. You will learn its secret when you go to the Spanish Steps tomorrow morning. There you will find Ariana."

Cara went back to the convent but that night, instead of dreams of palms and purity, she was assailed by a nightmare of a serial killer with a hangman's noose who stalked her into terrified wakefulness.

"Even in this sanctuary, I am not safe," she cried. "I must have the necklace. Its secrets will save me. Besides, it's valuable; if I need to, I can sell it."

Early next morning, even before breakfast and long before the tourist crowds, Cara set out for the center of Rome. No sooner had she arrived than she hurriedly began climbing the curved, down-slanted Spanish Steps towards the obelisk and twin-spired church of the Trinità dei Monti at the top.

Halfway up, she saw an elegant, blond woman cloaked in an ivory cashmere shawl descending toward her. She could have been Cara's younger sister, even Cara herself twenty-five years ago.

"Ariana," the woman introduced herself spontaneously. "And you must be Cara. You've come so early, eager to learn the secrets of the necklace. I am here to tell you about them. Listen closely." She sat down on a ledge where the steps curved up past the house in which the English poet Keats had died so young, at only twenty-five, his life suffocated by TB.

"There are those who believe in past lives. And future ones. It is said that, together, all these lives form an invisible necklace, each strand, a separate life. The prime of each life is relative," Ariana said, glancing towards the Keats plaque. "Those who are wise revere each present moment, each current life, as a precious link, not to be sullied or severed, but lived out in full measure. To play God and take it prematurely would be a sacrilege," she said meaningfully.

Cara looked away, embarrassed. How could this stranger have known of my ultimatum? And anyway what business is it of hers? Besides, how did she get the necklace? Amyra must have given it to her last night, but in fact it's mine, my life, a childish resentment rising inside her, resisting Ariana's good intentions.

She eyed the necklace and its double-helixed strands, the precious gemstones interspersed with semi-precious ones, as well as some others that were clearly nothing more than lusterless stones. But altogether, they formed a living entity, the strands wrapped around one another like vines. This necklace must be worth a lot. Aren't those precious stones? If I just removed the ruby, that diamond there… Cara was calculating when Ariana interrupted her thoughts.

"As for the gemstones on the necklace, it is not so much the precious ones, the hard, glittering diamonds, as the birthstones and natural pearls that are most sacred. For the beauty of these pearls—*the Enlightenment Stones*—lies in their wisdom that is born of the pain of gradual transformation. When a foreign grain of sand irritates the soft interior of the oyster, a pearl of wisdom grows around it as protection. There are many pearls on your invisible necklace of life. But also other dangerous stones. For you, dear Cara, there are three much-coveted stones you must give up. They must be replaced—for your own good—before the necklace can be entrusted to you. Look now and see which ones they are."

Ariana held up the glowing necklace, twirling it slowly in the sunlight. Cara watched it, fascinated, as the soft morning light caressed the many interwoven strands. Suddenly, "There!" she pointed. A bright, sparkling rhinestone all but blinded her.

"That is the *Exile's Stone*," said Ariana. "Flashy as all the places Cara visits—Paris, Hong Kong, New York, Geneva and, yes, even Rome—but empty and devoid of value. Never *home*. You need one with the hearth fire burning inside, like your birthstone, the opal."

With sudden insight, Cara recognized her attachment to such high-profile places: cities steeped in luxury but unable to sustain her questing inner life. She tried to imagine letting it go, replacing it with an iridescent opal.

Ariana twirled the necklace again and Cara quickly caught sight of a shiny obsidian stone sagging on the strand, pulling it down.

"That is the *Enslavement Stone*, that black-hole stone of achievement. It sucks everything into itself, makes work a Sisyphus addiction rather than a satisfaction. For those who are career-obsessed, it squeezes hard, then discards them. You must get free of enslavement—otherwise, its weight will break the strand and scatter all the stones."

Cara felt the powerful burden of the stone, imagined how it might be to relinquish its dark magnetism, replacing it by another lighter, irregular but natural pearl.

"That's better already," said Ariana. "But you still have a last stone on the strand of this life that is the most dangerous one of all. To find it, you'll have to consult Alessandra of Tivoli. That is beyond my realm. *The triad will take you to her.* Now I must go," she said and with that, Ariana swept her shawl around her—and vanished.

"Triad? What triad?" Hardly were the words out of her mouth when she spied them, three American women, engaged in animated conversation and mounting the steps towards her.

"Yes, and we were told we must rush to find her here and take her to—" said the tiny woman in their midst to the tall, slim one next to her.

"Oh, there she is!" interrupted the latter, taking the third by the arm and gliding over to where Cara stood mid-way up the Spanish Steps.

"Mornin', honey. I'm Mary, here's Maggie, and this is Myrna," said the smallest of the three in a lovely, long-drawn-out Southern drawl. "Now forgive me, but if my intuition serves me true, you're Cara."

"Well, yes, but..."

"And you're looking for the necklace. We know," interjected Myrna, a stunning petite brunette with sparkling blue eyes and obviously an avid necklace-lover.

"Not just the necklace," broke in blond, willow-slender Maggie. "Cara has important work to do. It's Alessandra she needs. *Andiamo. Volare! Eh, come me piace parlare italiano.* We'll have to arrange duty travel in Italy more often."

Together, they encircled her and the next instant, Cara found herself no longer on the Spanish Steps but in luxuriant gardens adorned with fountains everywhere she looked.

Walking along the pathways of fine white gravel, she heard footsteps behind her. "Tivoli," said a soft voice. "I thought you might like it here, with these fountains, these gardens full of springtime scents. I am Alessandra."

Cara turned. In the midst of a bower of fragrant, lavender-blooming wisteria, was a woman in her middle years, the laugh lines around her eyes attesting to a well-lived life. The eyes themselves were deep brown in a lovely face framed by shiny black hair. Kindness encircled her like an aura.

"No fountains of youth, these," she said, gesturing towards the nearest, "for all earthly bodies grow old and will one day perish. Trying to remain young is futile. No, these are inner healing fountains that wash away perceived sins, cleanse us of guilt that otherwise seduces and destroys us. If used well, they bestow greater gifts than borrowed youth: those of peace and the harmony of spirit that opens the door to real relationship."

These words, spoken so softly, reverberated around Cara. Then the surrounding fountains found another source; tears began to trickle down her cheeks, then overflow as she surrendered into Alessandra's waiting arms.

"I feel so exiled in this empty world of achievement I've created," Cara cried. "It's time to end it all. My life is a failure!"

"Then let it go—your *old* life," answered Alessandra, taking the hem of her white linen dress, dipping it in the water of the fountain, and dabbing away Cara's tears. "I know it's not easy. You have been severely wounded and burned. I saw it all in this fire coral." With that, she held the necklace aloft. "Do you see it?"

Cara looked, searched the strand as it revolved, suspended in the air from Alessandra's fingertips. Then she saw it, the jagged, livid crimson coral, its sensuality beckoning like the sirens but with sharp edges that cut deep, infected, wouldn't heal.

"The coral seems beautiful, alluring, but it's so sharp, it will sever the strand. You must let go of this *Exploitation Stone* that carries your sexual abuse and self-inflicted isolation. You cannot heal until you do. Return to Sister Angelica at the convent. It is she who has been entrusted with your necklace."

Alessandra embraced her warmly and, even as she did so, dissolved into the fragrant air of the Tivoli Gardens, leaving behind her only the scent of delicate wisteria.

Cara was alone in the garden, her own Gethsemane, sensing that life as she knew it would soon end. Only the precious necklace held out hope for her. "I must have it," she said to herself. Turning with determination, she left the ephemeral beauty that was Tivoli and headed back to the Eternal City, arriving just at dusk.

Ringing the convent bell, she stood outside and watched once again as the first time. Responding to her call, the doors swung slowly open on their silent hinges and she entered the sanctuary, going straight to the chapel illuminated with votive candles. There was Sister Angelica, just finishing vespers. She seemed to sense Cara's presence and turned to face her, the aged brown eyes behind her spectacles warm with wisdom.

"Welcome," she said simply. In her hand, next to her rosary, was Cara's necklace, its many lives interwoven in the double-helix of birth and rebirth.

"I've come for my necklace," Cara answered, forgetting to return the greeting. "Alessandra told me it was with you, but I must have it. It is *my* life. I can't entrust it to anyone, not even you."

"Of course, my child, it is yours. We are here only to protect you and to keep the necklace whole. This life's strand is in danger from those three stones you have seen. You must—"

But before the tiny Sister could finish, Cara reached out impetuously and wrested the precious necklace right out of Angelica's hands.

"Mine!!" spat a deep, guttural voice not at all like Cara's, as she fastened it around her neck.

But as she clutched it to her throat, she gasped. The jagged coral cut sharply into her flesh, drawing blood. In the same moment, she felt the necklace as a choker, tight as a noose around her neck.

Can't breathe! was her last sensation before she blacked out.

Whoever fought then—angels, dark demons—Cara was caught up in a physical, though unseen, battle that rocked the room around her. The struggle endured minutes, hours—eternity.

When at last this Armageddon was over, she came to, prone on the chessboard squares of the marble floor. The first sight she saw was Sister Angelica standing protectively over her, holding both her rosary, which remained intact, and Cara's necklace—but the strand that held her present life had been torn asunder. The stones had scattered, rolling out of control, bouncing in total disarray, echoing on the hard marble.

Suddenly, a passage from the German mystic poet, Rainer Maria Rilke, flashed across Cara's mind about moments of deepest revelation when *'something new enters into us, something unknown; then our feelings grow mute...everything in us withdraws, a stillness comes, and the new, which no one knows, stands in the midst of it and is silent.'*

Cara rose but remained motionless, suspended in time. Then, without a word, she knelt and began to pick up the pieces of her life's necklace, wrapping the broken strand and separate stones into a tissue.

The rhinestone, obsidian and coral she held separately, careful not to cut herself again. Now she took them, one by one, held them up to the candlelight, looked deeply into them, then put them down, all three, on the altar and turned to face Sister Angelica, who nodded, her eyes filled with tears.

Together now, they mended and lengthened the strand, gathered the scattered stones, and strung them. Cara noticed that now there were two additional pearls, the new ones shining softly next to a third stone, an iridescent opal, in the middle.

They worked long into the night. At last, Cara held her life's invisible necklace, mended. Still, it kept its secrets. To others, it would be a simple pearl rosary, but one that glowed, even in darkness.

By the time they had completed the task, the bells of St. Peter's were tolling two. Sister Angelica smiled wearily and, rising stiffly, came around to Cara, reached up and put the rosary around her neck.

"I am not worthy," she murmured as Cara embraced her and Someone somewhere smiled.

Trastevere

by Terry Brooks

I find the coat abandoned in the middle of a small side street in the *Trastevere* district of Rome on an April Sunday morning that is so bitterly cold it feels like winter has sent spring packing. The coat has an elegant look, long and tapered at the waist, sleeves and collar ringed with dark fur or something intended to approximate it. The position of the coat suggests it was attempting to flee under rather desperate circumstances. One sleeve is thrown across its body as if it had made a last futile attempt at saving itself before it was brought down. The other stretches towards the shuttered windows and doors of the surrounding buildings, seeking sanctuary.

Of course, a coat cannot flee or try to save itself. But it has that look about it. I can imagine it happening. I can envision its frantic efforts to escape from whatever pursued it. I can feel its final moments of panic just by looking at the way in which it sprawls upon the concrete. I don't need to know if it had an owner to lend it the attributes of a separate life.

Nevertheless, I glance at the surrounding buildings. No doors or windows are open, and no faces peek out from behind curtains. It is the Sunday before Easter, and most people are in church. Whoever left the coat is not looking for it. I glance around some more. No clotheslines are in evidence, so it does not appear that it was blown down in a high wind. Perhaps it fell out of a car or off a careless arm. But shouldn't someone have missed it by now?

Others from our little group join me. We are writers who have come to Rome to conduct an experimental writing program for the Maui Writers School. Over the course of a week, five of us will mentor another three dozen, using Rome and her people as inspiration for new prose. No one is allowed to bring anything old to the table. Everything must be written here, fresh and raw and spontaneous.

This morning, in preparation, mentors, spouses and significant others are touring three sights that will provide the anticipated inspiration for this coming week's efforts. It will help us as mentors to become familiar with the places we will visit over the next seven days. It will make us better prepared to offer advice. So the reasoning goes. Mostly, I find it is making me frozen and miserable.

Those with me have different responses to the coat on the ground. Some fail to notice it at all. Some notice it and think little of it beyond the obvious. Some, like myself, ponder its meaning and consider its significance. Different responses from different people—it is exactly what you would expect. I know it will be like this with those I will be mentoring. They will see the same sights, but their reactions to what they see will be entirely different.

My goal as mentor is to help my charges understand the importance of using reality as a springboard for the imagination. By looking around at the world, at its people, places and events, a writer's imagination should take flight. I learned some years ago as a young writer coming into the business that the time spent thinking about what I would write and how I would write it was every bit as important as the writing itself. I want those I mentor in Rome to understand this, too. I will stress it in my discussions with them. When they come to places like *Trastevere* for inspiration, they should take time to look around and dream about possibilities. They should think before they write. It is a hard lesson to teach and a hard lesson to learn. Impatience rules us. But time spent in reflection is invaluable. Thus, when they are finished, I want them to be able to explain how they got from what they saw to what they wrote.

We leave *Trastevere* and move on. But the following morning, I am back again. My group has drawn the district as its first stop. It is every bit as cold and gray and miserable now as it was the day before. Trastevere is a neighborhood for painters and craftsmen, and its piazzas and streets are their gathering places. Not on this morning, however. Not an artist is in sight, which I attribute to good sense, given the weather. (I will later discover that nothing is open on Monday mornings, in any case.) But I gather my charges about and give them their marching orders, sending them out to view and be inspired by the piazzas and churches and shuttered storefronts. Sometimes, waiting for the muse to appear is futile; you simply have to get out there and track her down.

My group disperses while I, rather hurriedly, walk to where I found the coat lying in the road yesterday morning.

It is gone, of course, as I suspected it would be. Coats lying on the ground attract attention. Someone would have picked it up. Perhaps the owner returned to find it or a neighbor recognized it and took it inside for safekeeping or one of the Gypsies that wander the city spirited it away.

Then again, it might not have needed to rely on humans. It might have gotten up all by itself after I left and simply gone on to wherever it had been headed all along. It might have been sleeping or unconscious while I was looking at it. It might even have been awake, playing possum to avoid drawing attention, hoping I would pass by. Once I was safely out of sight, off it went. Maybe it could fly. Maybe it did have an owner, and its owner was a spirit creature, a child of the wind, as substanceless as air, and the coat was its skin and its home in the world.

The possibilities are endless. The fact of the abandoned coat is all a writer's imagination requires in order to determine the truth of things. I was told once upon a time that E.L. Doctorow, when asked about his research for his period histories, said that a single sentence from any given time should be all a writer requires to create a story. Whether he said it or not, it is a great line.

I want the writers I work with this week to put that line to work for them. I want them to find their own coats upon the ground. I want them to find their own truths.

It is what writers do.

Quo Vadis – Reflections on a Pilgrimage to Rome
by Mark E. Prose

The turmoil and vagaries of life had drawn me to Rome. Having recently experienced a major life-changing event, my wife of twenty-five years passing away after a valiant fight with cancer, I was ready for something different. Instead of being a test of faith, the experience had been an affirmation of the joys of life and the importance of a faith well founded and supported. Together we learned to live each day as if it were our last, while being joyful of our many blessings. The love and support we received from all of our family and friends was uplifting and gratifying.

The opportunity to go to Rome, especially during Holy Week, was one of those moments in life that should not be passed up. The visit to the Eternal City and the Vatican came at a time of significant trials and tribulations for the Catholic Church, both in Rome and especially in the United States. Many are upset with "The Church" and express displeasure—and in some cases hatred—of this or that aspect of "The Church." Listening to the comments of some of the participants provided a mere glimpse of the depth and passion of these feelings and perceptions. The same is true from listening to the complaints within my parish and diocese.

The common thread I find in all of these discussions is that people are upset with the actions or conduct of individuals, whether they be priests, bishops, other religious or lay ministry personnel. Standing at the center of Christianity and the Catholic Church, it is hard to imagine there is such a storm raging around it and yet such has been the situation throughout history. The Catholic Church has not thrived and survived throughout the centuries because of any given individuals, but has survived in spite of some of them, because the basic teachings and core values of Jesus Christ are the heart and soul of the faith.

Most problems have been the result of individuals putting personal interests ahead of the greater good and message of Christ. The schism between the Eastern Rite and Western Rite was the result of power struggles between individuals, such as Lombard Cardinal Humbert and Patriarch Michael Cerularius, who used meaningless issues to divide the visible Church on earth. The Reformation was the result of significant and in may cases obscene excesses and abuses by individuals in positions of power. St. Francis led the way in pointing out how many had strayed from the principles of Christ's teachings. Unfortunately these warnings were ignored and greater conflicts arose, as others used these abuses to justify their own agendas, some of which were equally selfish. The splintering continues in America at an almost exponential pace, as various ministries are founded based on the disgruntled feelings and charisma of ministers and cult founders.

One conference member complained of the actions of the "Ghetto Church" which only took from the members of the community and put nothing back into the community. The only message heard was "Give, give, give!" Another member complained of a lack of reasoning in dealing with a family reaching the point of too many mouths to feed and talked of the individual being excommunicated (which is never actually done in such situations) because of a desire to utilize birth control methods. These issues reflect a lack of understanding, pragmatism and a legalistic view of the faith and the

Church. All of us should be constructively engaged in the affairs of the Church, hold the "shepherds" accountable and not be victims. For example, in our parish, an effort is underway to remodel and renovate the facilities. The capital campaign has not gone well because many do not like the way the pastor has taken care of his personal wants first at the expense of some real parish needs. That does not mean we have stopped giving to "The Church." Instead many of us, independently, contribute to other areas of "The Church," such as Catholic Charities or other worthy charities. When hit in the collection basket, the pastor starts to take notice, as does the bishop, and responds. The response may not be to our full liking, but they are responding.

Many of us are confident enough in our faith to realize that our relationship with God does not depend upon what our pastor thinks of our disagreement with him. If the parishioners in the "Ghetto Church" had taken such actions, one would hope that their pastor and bishop would have been perceptive enough to realize what the problem was. Even so, both should have focused on support of the "Ghetto Church" instead of taking from the parish. Instead, a victim mentality was allowed to develop, at least among some of the parishioners, to the point where they drifted away from the faith or remain bitter members of the Church. The same is true for the situation concerning birth control and excommunication. Some narrow-minded parish priest may have thoughtlessly used such an expression, but the reality is that it is a matter of conscience between the individual and God. The Church teaches the ideal, but individuals must work out the practical aspects of life. Again, one must have true confidence in their faith and not get wrapped up in the legalistic aspects of the Church. Form is not a substitute for true faith. And true faith does not require a formulary approach to the teachings of the Church.

As we stood in the Papal audience, I heard some conference members express shock and disgust with some of the enthusiastic greetings for John Paul II. They took it as inappropriate adoration. But they were judging it from their own cultural perspective and their prejudical view of "the Church." From their North American perspective, they fail to realize that many of the faithful throughout the rest of the world view John Paul II as a true hero. Eastern Europeans, and many Western Europeans, recognize the significant part John Paul II played in the peaceful end of the Cold War and the collapse of the Iron Curtain. Most recognize that John Paul II was not the only player, but the force of his moral authority helped to pave the way for a rapid and near bloodless demise of the communist empire.

Standing under the canopy of the Sistine Chapel ceiling, admiring the glory and splendor Michelangelo envisioned, I could not help but be inspired. Some say that the Church should sell off all of its treasures and property and use the proceeds to help the poor around the world. To what end? Such an action would bring immense pleasure to those who do not like the Church and would like to see its physical presence erased. But it would bring only momentary relief to some small fraction of those considered "poor" or "unfortunate". The same could be suggested of the treasures within the Smithsonian Institute. An example of the real and most effective work of the Church is the worldwide efforts of Mother Theresa and her nuns. Individual face-to-face work has a more direct and positive effect than wasteful "gifts." The physical presence of the Church is only meant to inspire the spirit, and to provide peaceful solitude and sanctuary for the restless soul. Those who do not like the Church do not fully understand that the physical presence of the Church is not just the buildings, but the people, the faith community. At the Easter Vigil Mass I could feel the spirit of this faith community even though I could not speak the languages of most of those present.

Some criticize the form, pomp and circumstance of the Mass, but it is precisely this that unites all of us in the faith community. Those with an open mind can see that between the Eastern and Western Rites there are only minor differences in the Mass, and none of these differences detract from the overriding significance and ultimate importance of the celebration of the Eucharist. In this respect we are still united. The breaking of the bread and mixing of water with wine are not just symbols and reminders of the Last Supper, but rather a full and total connection with Christ through time. This is what connects all of us together, not just our baptism, but our active participation in the Eucharist. It is not just the act, but the mental effort required to participate that matters. As the many thousands of us took Communion this joyous evening, we once again affirmed our faith in the risen Christ and the promise of the Resurrection.

Our visits to the Catacombs and Pompeii were a powerful reminder of the trials, tribulations and spirit of the early Church, and the fleeting temporal nature of life. Pompeii, a vibrant city gone in an instant, demonstrates how little control we have over some events, and serves as a humbling reminder that each of us is here for a relatively short period of time. Make the most of your time and talents while you can. Some people are caught up in the minutia of everyday things (how many pages to a chapter, how many chapters to a book, how much will I make from this contract or deal, what do I get out of this, etc.) and miss the simple needs of others. Within the six months prior to this trip two people very close to me passed away. It is with joy that I can say they had lives well lived. They were not famous, but they touched many in a very positive way with their quiet and exemplary service to others. Note that the emphasis is on service. Standing before the tomb of Saint Peter, the best I can wish for is that others may someday say the same of me. And so, where are *you* going?

Keats' Last Letter

by Sandra Loera

How long is this posthumous life of mine to last?
—Keats
February 23, 1821

Hamstead,
November 30th, 1820

My Sweet Girl,

This is the first letter you receive, my dearest Fanny, but know that I have spoken to you ever before within my mind where you are and will always be. Only a need to speak to the one person who will hear me has made me break my long silence. I left to keep you from the pain of sharing in these, my last days. They are long without you, but otherwise they are not without comfort.

I was right to leave England. The good Dr. James Clark who was well recommended to me has discovered me to be suffering from stomach ailments and has suggested long walks to which Rome is much better suited than England. Severn and I have found the public walk on the *Pincio* to be sheltered from the north wind making our sojourns warm as a summer's day.

The streets of Rome call to me. Alive as they are, they accost all my senses and refuse to be ignored. At times I must shut my eyes to relieve them of the necessity of seeing another masterpiece or a pair of eyes to inspire me. Last month, I felt compelled to be on my own. My good friend, without intending to, has been my keeper in so many ways that at times I feel imprisoned by more than my illness. Thus, when Severn reluctantly left to meet a business associate, I stepped from our building with such glee and abandonment as might befit a small child. I took to a path not yet traveled with any friend and soon came upon one of the myriad of small piazzas which both bless and curse Rome. I decided to rest before finding my way back, for I had to admit that I had come perhaps too far and was more tired than I had been for several weeks.

There, I spied two actors attempting to entertain passersby. I was pleased to be again enjoying the artists of the streets. They were performing a drama filled with pathos and humor; their costumes rich in color and texture. I laughed to see them. The actors were somewhat of a distance from me. When my eyes shifted, I could see their audience pass in front of me. Some passed by with great disdain saying with a sneer upon their faces, "What is this? Surely you do not suggest this is art?" Others simply passed by. My fellow artists did not exist for their audience, and whatever these passers by might be trying to say was of no consequence to them. Some, my dear Fanny, took pity upon the artists and dropped a coin into their purse. Pity was the most these actors could hope for.

Before my eyes appeared all the artists that have come before, all the singers, painters, jugglers and—I must force myself to say—poets. Fanny, I saw myself. Who is to say that my poetry is not one and the same as these artists? Where will my printed word be tomorrow? Influential friends to whom I am much indebted have brought my work to print. These Romans are without such friends; can this be all that separates us?

Sitting in the piazza, I suffered a fear so great that it

has not left me still. It is as much that as my illness that has created a chill no fire has been able to warm. Fanny, forgive me, but you—at least—must know the truth. I can speak it to no one else though I have tried. All refuse to listen. My friends will tell you that this fever has left me weak. That it is the fever that has stilled my pen. It is ever more true, however, that the walk in which I indulged myself has left me unable to leave this room, this fire.

You and I are connected beyond the borders of the England and Rome that separate us. I write to you, that you may not doubt what I feel you must know—even when all will tell you differently. I do not fear death, Fanny. I welcome its nearness. The fear of having lost that which has given me life is great within me. Do not remember me in pity.

Yours Ever,
J. Keats

Fanny returned the letter to its accustomed folds and replaced it gently into her apron pocket. She walked the wooded path that circled the more formal garden. At the crest of the hill she looked across the newly green hills to the cherry trees beginning to flower. How can it be that Spring has remembered to bloom? Is it possible that this same sun continues to rise, to shine, to bring forth life? Her thoughts circled round in an angry cloud through which she now saw all things. Only these same walks brought her any peace and even they seemed to mock her.

The first spring without Keats. Fanny stood on the path that she had last shared with him. She plucked a single leaf. Alone without sympathies, without advice, Fanny felt him all around her. The afternoon before he left for Rome, he held her to him. Here. He stood here. He was unaccustomedly cheerful, willing her to be the same. He took her face in both his hands. "Fanny, my great love for you takes me physically from you. Yet, you and I will never part for I must take you with me even to Rome."

Fanny did not argue as she had on so many occasions. It was too late for he would leave within the hour and she had no means to follow. Fanny had only her love to recommend her. She had almost convinced him that her love was strong enough to share even death with him. Her love more than any climate could cure him. A month, a year, a day together were worth more than any lifetime apart. Alone she could convince him.

But they were seldom alone. Her mother, without a word, won her argument, for she was ever the young widow struggling through life, dependent on the generosities of family and friends. His mother's death followed so closely by that of his brother haunted him with a freshness never lost in eight years. Letters from Shelly and Byron were filled with the romance of their exiles in Italy. Charles and the doctors warned that another winter in England would be too great a danger. Throughout, Fanny had always believed that whether England or Italy, she and Keats would be together.

Severn. Today he returns to England to everyone's admiration, the good friend. Severn, whose letters to everyone but Fanny, shared his suffering as he nursed his friend. Severn's letters telling of sitting with Keats to his last moments, of keeping laudanum from him in his last days, of hearing his last words.

The house had become unbearable as it filled with preparations for Severn. The others did not ask her to help because they understood her grief. In actuality, she welcomed activity, craved it. Something to take her mind and her heart from the absence of Keats. But she would do nothing to prepare for Severn. If she could prevent his return, she would put all her energies there. For he was returning without Keats, as she knew he must. He was also returning as the instrument who tied Keats to

those who loved him. He was bringing a promised painting of Keats to Charles. Charles, whose friendship was
pure, longed for the portrait to remind him of his friend.

Fanny understood. She too longed for a talisman of
her departed friend. Everything of his had been burned
by the Italians in a hopeless fight against the spread of
the consumption. Everything. Had he written to her? Did
the Italians burn a last letter? Or was it Severn, as she
was more willing to believe. No letters. One to Charles
written the same morning as hers. Mailed when Severn
was away for a day.

Perhaps only one lover can recognize the acts of another. Keats would not have left her unless convinced
that it was proof of greater love to leave, to spare her.
Rome. So far away, so impossible to follow. In Rome,
Severn could keep Keats to himself. Do all for him. Become all to him. His jealousy and greed kept Keats' last
laborious breath to himself.

Fanny had been unable to fight against Severn, for
he was an experienced lover. He used Keats' love for
Fanny to win his departure. Her passion had been too
great to allow her to see the real enemy until he had won
and Keats had gone away. In the long months since their
departure, Fanny saw that Severn must win for his was
not only a fight to gain love, but to salvage his medioc-
rity. He would associate himself forever with the genius
of Keats. Perhaps he would be granted a poem to equal
his love or perhaps a line, a word of gratitude to immor-
talize him.

Fanny dropped the leaf now crushed within her palm.
She felt the letter close to her heart. The sound of the
carriage arriving below flashed in her ears. She kept to
the path not hurrying her step. She walked with Keats
now as she would every day of her life. She felt the warm
breeze around her and again felt his hand upon her cheek.

Once within the parlor, she smiled at Severn and extended her hand. "I have thought of you often with great pity," she said.

Severn bowed and cast down his eyes accepting her condolence.

A Many Splendored Thing
by Kathryn Mattingly

Swishing red *vino* in a stemmed glass, she saw him from across the room. His attractive form quickened the beat of her traitorous heart as she downed the Merlot. Catching a glimpse of his shadow hovering near, she beckoned the barmaid for a refill. She held her breath and wondered what he was thinking as he sat opposite her, revealing a fire in his eyes that slowed her pulse. Not an ounce of seduction oozed from him, the lack of it seducing her brazenly.

She dropped her vision from smoldering eyes to warm smile, and then to his beautiful, strong hands folded on the table. All of him was reflected in those hands, and she longed to touch them, trace his fingers with her own, pick each one up and caress it gently... kissing every tip.

Instead she cupped the stemmed glass of newly poured *vino* and waited, poised to sip on sin. Breathless with anticipation, she watched the barmaid pour his, leaving the bottle and a backward glance with one raised brow and half a smile.

Nodding often and laughing freely, she listened to him talk while hungrily inhaling scents of bread baking, pasta boiling, tomatoes simmering in a steel pot. It was intoxicating, intuitively knowing his feelings for her. Did he know hers as well? She thought perhaps he did, but they did not speak of it, being only friends and behaving as friends should behave. His way with words was music for her mood, non-threatening casual words that made her eyes dance as his resonant voice broke her heart with wanting.

Soon piano keys were thumping and a merry tune enticed them to the dance floor. Sweet heavy scents hugged the air as they moved with the music. They touched carefully as friends would touch, laughed heartily as friends would laugh. But then the music slowed and the room swayed. He caught her gently and held her snug against his chest, his head on top of hers. Quietly they danced by dim light in the smoke-filled room. Sharp images filled her hazy head. The cheating on her mind could not be dulled.

It carried her out the door, purse in one hand, coat in the other. Fresh air filled her lungs. Spicy aromas lingered in the crisp night air. Stars shimmered overhead and their sharp twinkling burned clear through her as he put his arm around her shoulder. Could he walk her to her room? She whisked down the cobbled street, no reply escaping from her lips. But he stayed protectively near, held her coat, and when she faltered, held her arm.

She crossed the side street, found the flat that housed her things, and leaned against its cool bricks. Her back against the rough surface, she breathed deeply while looking up at the twinkling stars staring down. They were dancing a dizzy waltz when his face appeared between her and the heavens, shining down on her sorry state. She was in love with this man and didn't want to be. Raging against the irresistible power of it, reveling in the sublime taste of it, she was too weak to push away her feelings and yet too strong to allow the consequences.

Feeling his warmth only weakened her resolve, as did the resonant voice inquiring if she was all right. His distinctive features illuminated by the moon straight above were not classical in design but a concerto to her, arousing volumes of glorious wishing. Slowly, hesitantly, she raised her hands and touched his face, thinking she saw a glimmer of longing in his expression. Pulling him to her, she gently kissed his lips. He lingered there for an eternal second, and then hungrily kissed her back. No denial. No hesitation. As if he had waited patiently for this.

And now what? Should she bring him up the flight of stairs beyond the entry, down the narrow hall to her cozy rented room? Or leave him hovering there, while slipping delicately from his grasp, to greet her bed alone and face tomorrow sober, more the victor for her fortitude?

It was buried at the bottom of the trunk, a little black leather-bound book. *Journal* was engraved across the front, and when the child opened the cover, her heart sang with delight. The words there had been written freehand by her grandmother. Bringing the book with her, the nearly grown child climbed into the wooden swing and gave it a gentle push. She looked up and squinted into the sun as a warm wind tickled her face and teased the floppy straw hat on her grandmother, in the garden across the yard. The twelve-year-old was pleased to see her glance over and smile approval for the discovered treasure.

The faded ink on yellowed paper revealed descriptions and observations of Rome, noted in the journal as the eternal city. But most exciting to the grandchild were the pages that spoke of love, not for family and friends, but that other kind of love that was slowly awakening within her. Never having been to a foreign city and longing for such an adventure of her own, she greedily inhaled the words written on thin worn pages from many years past.

Entry for March 25th
I have met someone who causes me to be unfaithful in my heart. We sit at the outside cafes in the Piazza Navona and

*drink strong cappuccinos while discussing our photography. I
don't hear his wonderful insight into lenses, I only hear his
deep resounding voice that beckons me to take the most amazing pictures of my life. It is not the class that has taught me so
well, but my heart that inspires me to see everything more viv-
idly. The men and women in the fountains have come alive,
their emotion-filled faces not just etched stone, but more com-
pelling than the beautiful marble that defines them. I think of
loved ones back home and wish to share this magic scene. But
part of me is grateful for the distance between us, the part of
me selfishly seeking a friendship that harbors feelings too risky
to chance.*

Entry for March 26th

*Today we discover the wonderful scents and brilliant col-
ors of* Campo di Fiore. *Fruit and vegetable vendors shout in
melodious tones of their native Italian. I delight in the busy
arena of the marketplace filled with shoppers in black leather
on this crisp late March day. We meander down the same narrow cobbled street to snap our frames of art. Our laughter echoes off the buildings and comes back to us, like a shadow of
guilt clinging to my mind. I cannot help myself from wanting
more and more time alone with him. We carefully slip away
from the group we are with to learn about our craft. Expertise
in photography is less important than sharing steaming plates
of fresh pasta in a small café. We have a bottle of wine and
linger long beyond the designated time to reunite with other
students. Sitting too close together in the back of a cab we are
quiet, our heavy thoughts surrounding us like fog enveloping
the city.*

Entry for March 27th

*This morning our class visits the Sistine Chapel and St.
Peter's Cathedral. Everywhere I look there are well-preserved
erotic and religious paintings depicting love as either sensual
or divine. The profound power of this art tugs at my heart and
makes it ache, while stolen glances between my special friend
and I overwhelm it with joy. Love is, as the song would sug-*

gest, a many splendored thing. It is odd to call love a 'thing' ...yet it can often rear its ugly head. Everywhere I look I see that love has not only been savored, but lives have been severed due to this 'thing' called love. I attribute this in part to the fact it is not a 'thing' we have control over. In the end you cannot fool your heart. It beats for whom it wishes, and you are the victim of its choosing. You can accept it or rail against it, but you cannot change it.

Entry for March 28th

Back in my hotel room I have looked up splendor and found it to mean a multitude of things such as magnificent, brilliant, a great brightness or luster. Is that not what love is? Love sharpens the senses, pierces the darkness, and awakens our joy. Truly, it is amazing how these positive adjectives and intense feelings that bring purpose and meaning to life can also get us into so much misery and trouble. And if love is all of these wondrous things, how can it also at times be such a vile and bloodsucking monster, clawing through our veins in the form of lust, and causing us to lose our common sense, if not our virtue? I think love is not a choice, it is a destiny. Not an act of will, but an act of fate. And when you find yourself in the throes of it, there is little you can do.

Entry for March 29th

I have held his hand in the dark tunnels of the catacombs. We have stood side by side in awe of the Colosseum, and everywhere we go our hearts and minds soak up the beautiful sculptures and canvases, thirsty for the meaning and purpose behind each one. The feelings that we share give depth to the ecstasy and agony of emotion felt in the history and art of this eternal city, where this 'thing' called love has made murderers of poets, drawn tears from bullies, strengthened the weak, dropped kings to their knees. I have learned that nothing is more debilitating, more coveted or more frightening, more incredible or more difficult to understand, than love. It distinguishes men from beasts and makes beasts of men. It encompasses all that life is, drives the very core of our needs and is

what makes humanity work. Yet, love is indeed a many
splendored thing, and worth the price. Is it not?

The child wondered what price her grandmother had
paid for love. They locked eyes from across the yard and
burst into warm smiles. The young girl's heart was
flooded with happy memories of a grandmother she
thought she knew so well, yet barely knew at all. She
was someone to bake cookies with in the kitchen off this
porch the swing sat on. Or to play hide and seek with in
the garden where she now stood, looking almost young
and beautiful again. It was hard to imagine her grandmother having a past without her, yet their lives together
had begun long after the trip to Italy had turned into
memories as fragile as a glass slipper.

With bare toes dangling above the cool porch floor
the pre-adolescent was surprised by these pages filled
with troubled and confused feelings. They were not to
be expected from her grandmother who had always been
so strong and wise. The girl gave the wooden seat suspended by chain links a swift upward thrust and hoped
the final entry would give answers to this real life fairytale
of forbidden love.

Entry for March 30th

This is our last day in Rome together. In the morning we
will begin our journey home. We sit on the Spanish Steps and
stare at the monstrous billboard of painted fashions on the build-
ing facing us. No words come. The early morning chill, with-
out the sun to defy it on this day stifles our humor. We agree to
meet for dinner. Reluctantly we rise and make an effort to ex-
plore, feebly snapping gray distant shots of a sleepy city awak-
ening before our eyes. For the last time, we window shop side
by side. Our pictures are not fine art in the making, but of each
other, and strangers snapping us in many silly or somber poses
at our request. I can think of nothing but the dinner we have
agreed to have alone at a bar with music and dancing. I love to
dance. I am happily anticipating our evening together, but sad

at the indiscretion of my deviant plan. I should not be with this man, and I have no right to want him… to love him. But I cannot help myself.

What did her grandmother do? Did she dance with the mysterious prince? And if she did, and she truly loved this man, why did she run back to sweeping the ashes of her everyday life? Maybe the man in the story was her grandfather. Perhaps one day her grandmother would tell. But for now the spry little woman in the big floppy hat just smiled while watching from the petunia beds.

And the child not yet fully understanding the meaning of the words written in her grandmother's journal, only hoped that she would one day have a journal filled with her own secrets of the heart. Surely by then she would know if love were indeed a many splendored thing, worth the price.

The Plum

by Leah Tribolo

Sister Constanza's face was flushed red and sweat beaded her temple where the wimple covering her hair met skin. The black wool of her habit was hot and heavy, making the heat of summer an act of penance. Her ankles were swollen. Her feet hurt. She paused to catch her breath at the head of the alley adjoining the square where the hustle of the market began.

She not only needed to catch her breath but she also needed to brace herself to face the crowd of people. She had worked all night again in the hospice and was so tired. The sisters' labor never seemed to end or cause any lasting difference in the lives of the poor. They lived in misery and died in it. Constanza sighed with regret and observed the market. The market was overflowing with people, and sometimes laughter rose to her on a light breeze. The variety of produce in the stands amazed her; all the colors of the rainbow were represented by God's creations.

She turned her attention to the less fortunate lining the edges of the square and felt her heart clench. They were always there and more came everyday it seemed. She knew many of them by name from serving in the soup kitchen at the cloister. They did not have a lot of hope and there was little more she could do for them. They were silent for the most part; often sitting with a hand outstretched, hoping for a spare coin.

Constanza skimmed over them until her eyes stopped on an old man sitting not too far from her. He didn't fit in with the others. His shoulders were bent, but he still had hope. He looked familiar, sitting on the stairs of the fountain playing a tune on a battered guitar. He returned her gaze with a smile hovering around the edges of his mouth. His blue eyes seemed to glow and his white hair shone like a halo in the light of the golden sun.

She felt a tug at her skirt, then a mall voice from behind her said, "Please."

"I am sorry. I have nothing," Sister Constanza said as she turned to face him. He was small for his age. She felt her eyes fill with tears as she saw how his cheeks lacked the plumpness of childhood.

"They all say that," he said.

There are so many in need, she thought, God help them all, for I can't. Constanza noticed the holes in the boy's shirt and the smudges of grime layered onto his skin and concern for this boy rose within her overtired heart. "Where are your parents, boy?"

"Gone. I dunno," he said and shrugged.

"The church could take you in. They would find you a home. What is your name?"

"Why? Will they change anything?" the boy said, not bothering to name himself. He straightened his shoulders and targeted a group of housewives nearby with his sad eyes. "I will see if they have something to offer. Good-bye, sister."

"Please," she said going after the boy. She put a hand on his shoulder as if to turn him toward her. "We can help you, but you have to come with me."

He looked back at Constanza and glared. "I have heard stories about the church, no thanks," he said and continued on

"God bless," she called after the boy and felt her shoulders slump with her failure. There are so many people who need His blessing, she thought. We make no difference.

Constanza could make out a tune coming from the old man's guitar and moved closer to him. It was one she often heard on the organs in the church where she worshipped. He sat slouched over the body of the guitar with his long white hair hiding his face. His fingers danced over the strings, bringing forth a creation that compelled her to listen as it lifted her heart. When Sister Constanza made a move to leave, the man glanced up at her. His bright eyes peering out of their wrinkled caves pierced her soul with their intensity, forcing her to stay. Eventually he finished his song, gesturing for her to sit beside him.

Sister Constanza did not move. "Your music is very beautiful, a gift from God."

"Thank you. God has many better musicians than I, though, I won't deny that He has many gifts to give. Do you perhaps have a coin to spare?"

"I am sworn to poverty and carry nothing. I'm sorry," she replied with regret in her voice. "I will pray for you." It seems that is all I can do, she thought.

"Don't be sorry, sister, a prayer is more than one such as I could hope to receive. Let me give you this in token of my esteem." The man reached into the canvas bag sitting at his feet and pulled out a perfect purple plum for Constanza. She couldn't take her eyes off the plum as it shone in the afternoon light.

"I couldn't. It is your last one," Constanza said. "I have nothing to offer in return."

"Take it," he said, and gestured with the plum, "please. It is nothing and would mean a lot to me."

"I haven't had one since I was a child."

"Then all the more reason to, sister. There is more to this life than denial of it, and a plum is little enough."

Sister Constanza took the plum from his outstretched hand. She felt the smooth skin encircling the soft juicy flesh of the fruit underneath. Her mouth watered as she remembered the sensation of sweet juice bursting through the tight skin. "Thank you for your kindness."

"It is nothing," he said and turned back to his guitar. This time he sang along with his tune in a voice that although untrained sounded like an angel had touched it.

Constanza watched him for awhile considering her good fortune. Eventually she turned towards home and slipped the fruit into a voluminous pocket within her skirt. She walked through the market, hardly noticing the people.

The other side of the market opened onto the bank of the river. Sister Constanza paused to lean over the edge of the wall and gaze into the murky water. She slipped her hand into the pocket and felt the cool firm flesh of the fruit against the palm of her hand.

She could almost taste the plum from her childhood memories. The sticky sweet juice had dribbled down her chin and she slurped noisily as she tried to get all of the liquid before it dripped to the ground. Her father, bless him, loved to treat her to them. He bought them by the bag full and never took one for himself. He always said, "Seeing you eat them is pleasure enough, Constanza." She smiled at the memory of him and raised the plum toward her lips. How he had loved her.

Then her eye caught on the beggar boy she had spoken with earlier. He sat alone now, crouched on the ground leaning against an old building. He was staring at the crowd with an outstretched hand and appeal in his eyes, but no one stopped for him. No one seemed to see him—except her.

The plum felt heavy in her hand as her eyes rested on his hunched shoulders but her mouth still watered. Her fingers tightened on the taut purple flesh as she thought of the sensation of her teeth sinking into the sweetness. Constanza slowly lowered the plum and considered the nature of her vows.

Momma Mia

by Octavia Hudson

Emmanuel found out about his mother by accident, overhearing his father instructing Paulo, the bodyguard.

Through the bars of the embassy window overlooking the *Piazza Navona*, Emmanuel sees Paulo. He's parked along the *Via Della Cuciagna*, a side street jutting out from the piazza. It is still early, before the sun heats the morning chill. The throng of tourists and locals has not yet filled the piazza, hovering around Bernini's famous fountain of the four rivers.

Paulo sits in an idling BMW, waiting, watching. She's there too, looking like just another gypsy to ignore—dressed in black and wearing the pitiful look of an experienced beggar. Emmanuel's eyes search for something familiar. How can this woman be his mother? She looks too old, too discarded.

All day, Paulo watches her every move, as she hobbles on the black cobblestone with a cane, shaking her cup of coins at passing tourists. Emmanuel is afraid for her and afraid for himself. The son of a diplomat embracing a gypsy mother could wave his and his father's political careers good-bye. Emmanuel's eyes shift back and forth between the old woman and Paulo in the idling car.

His mind jumps back to Paulo and his father. The two had stopped talking when they realized he was listening. Paulo left the room when Emmanuel confronted his father. In the shock that shattered his heritage, Emmanuel had forgotten about Paulo. What had the Don instructed him to do?

From the embassy window above the piazza, Emmanuel sees Paulo pull something out of the glove compartment and put it on the seat. Knowing his father, Emmanuel knows the Don will not risk the scandal. Don Emmanuel Corteza is Brazil's ambassador to Rome from a prestigious family. Family. Family—the importance of family. It is a mantra burrowed deep into his brain and drilled deeper at every opportunity.

Twenty years ago his father had taken his namesake and sailed to Rome. "You are the image of your father. You look just like him." He had heard that all of his twenty years.

But he isn't like his father, cold, aloof, rigid with pride and disinterested in the steady flow of women that he uses to warm his bed. How could the Don have loved this woman? How could she leave her child? Emmanuel didn't believe the explanation that his father gave when confronted. The Don said that his mother had refused to nurse him, that she had discarded him. He didn't want to believe it.

Probably his father kidnapped him as a baby, tearing him away from his nursing mother, not willing to marry this common woman and not willing to give up the child that looked just like him. That sounds like his father. Possessed by his possessions.

Paulo moves again in the BMW, putting whatever he took out of the glove compartment into his pocket.

Emmanuel's eyes dart back to his mother. Did she just look up at him in the window? He imagines that she could not be as bad as she looks, stooped over her cane, her black scarf covering her head and most of her face. Why is she here? What does she want after twenty years? Emmanuel cannot stop the stream of questions flowing through his head.

All his life, his father had lied to him, told him his

mother died in childbirth. If he lied then, he's probably lying now. What is she like, this woman? Emmanuel imagines a loving mother who spent her life looking for her only son. He has always wanted a mother, craving to crawl into her warm embrace. As a child he'd watched his friends with their mothers—laughing, touching, soothing life's bruises.

The more Emmanuel imagines, the more his need draws him to the beggar woman in the piazza. He could get closer. Maybe talk to her. That wouldn't jeopardize his father's position. Plus he needs to make sure that she is safe from Paulo.

As usual, the tall, black embassy doors facing the piazza inch open. But today it is too slow for Emmanuel's impatience. He is ready to meet his mother. With the two doors still creeping apart, Emmanuel squeezes through on to the piazza.

She isn't at her usual place. Not at the fountain. Not in front of the towering St. Agnes Cathedral. Not in front of the outdoor cafes lining the piazza. Emmanuel's eyes search through the tourists meandering past the artists and their easels.

Then he spots her, walking toward him, standing straight, with her cane, her limp and her cup of coins gone. Her black scarf still covers her face. Emmanuel hesitates until he sees Paulo running toward his mother. Emmanuel starts running toward her too, intent on cutting off Paulo and whatever he is intending.

Too late. Emmanuel sees the mad satisfaction on her face too late, and he never sees the knife that pierces his skin and his illusions. Emmanuel recoils from flailing eyes that only register hatred. Paulo drags the woman away screaming, "Death to you Don Emmanuel. Death to you and our bastard child."

Lazy by Occupation
by Joni Barron Brotherton

Cynthia was tired and just a little bit angry as she nursed her cappuccino. She hadn't wanted to come to Rome with Roger and she hadn't wanted to go shopping with these ditsy women. For God's sake, she thought, all they talk about is their kids and shopping. She didn't have kids and would rather read a book than shop. Maybe she could get them into that little church on the piazza if they ever came out of that shoe store.

Cynthia did like people watching, however, and this little café on a narrow cobblestone street was a great place to watch the goings-on. And the Romans were so much fun to watch.

Much more interesting than the Midwestern college town where they all lived. Fulton, Missouri wasn't exactly the hot spot of culture or fashion. Westminster College was in Fulton and, as a college town, people thought they were dressed up when the men wore sport coats and the women wore tired navy blue or black dresses. Sometimes they changed the scarves or added pearls. Pretty risqué.

Cynthia had already seen lots of fashionable women clad in bowling shoes and long, solid-colored fringed scarves knotted around their necks. This was Roman chic. Not the kind of outfits that would play in Fulton, Cynthia mused.

Then Cynthia saw two men walking down the street

toward her. They began to settle in just down and across the street. They were purposeful, as if they had a mission.

It was like the old men back home that sat outside Cooper's Grocery daily, watching housewives and others go in and out. They seldom moved, but commented on the weather, the news, and gossiped. These two Roman men would have fit right in on the bench in Fulton, if only they spoke English.

They looked to Cynthia like they met at that same place on the street every day. For some reason it appeared they never agreed on anything. She could tell by looking.

The larger man was maybe five-foot ten and his weight had long since past chunkiness into a semi-solid mass of flesh that he had trouble keeping in place. His exact height was difficult for Cynthia to determine because of the way he sprawled in his chair. At least she assumed that there was a chair under him. He is like a cat, she thought, trying to position himself to catch the sun and warm himself in the early morning chill. He tilted back, clasping his hands behind his head and grunted with the effort of shifting and repositioning his feet to get the right balance to stay upright as he wiggled the chair legs.

It appeared necessary to move the chair a little in order for both his legs to warm in the sun. He looked experienced at jump-starting his chair to move it on the rough, cobbled Roman street. If he positioned himself just right it would probably be an easy half-hour before he'd have to move to either continue basking in the sun or shift to escape its heat. Cynthia knew it would be difficult to calculate how many times a day he needed to reposition himself. It seemed apparent that this was the regular hangout of *Signore* Big Man and his thin companion.

Just as the Big Man's corpulence gave room for description, the small man was nondescript. Cynthia couldn't come up with any distinguishing features. He was of indeterminate age, not wiry, merely scrawny. His face was lined with ordinary cares. Nothing of note had marked his life. But she bet that he joined the big man daily, sitting upright on a small wooden chair, shifting and angling himself to maintain his conversational position with his friend. What he contributed she couldn't imagine.

They sat close to one another so they could hear above the roar of a motorbike as it whizzed by. So close, but no one flinched. Neither the biker nor the men, all confident in their place in the world and laying down a cloak of daring to anyone who would disturb this well-executed system.

It dawned on Cynthia that it would never have occurred to the men to move further back against the wall bordering the narrow street. This was, after all, their place. And if they didn't move for the Vespas, they certainly didn't move for the inconvenient tourists who happened by.

They both were reading sections of the paper, commenting back and forth in such a way that they appeared to condense the news into the Italian equivalent of an "ain't it awful" conversation. As she watched them, before they had a chance to assess blame for the sorry condition of the world, their attention was drawn to noisy confusion down the street. They looked up from their papers to see several young people who had appeared about a half block down the road. Cynthia followed their eyes just in time to view the latest action on the street.

The men huddled as they watched to try to determine the purpose of the new goings-on they were witnessing. Neither seemed disturbed by their close proximity. God, their breath must reek of old coffee and rotten teeth, Cynthia thought, shuddering at the imagined smell. It was also obvious that bathing and clean clothes took a back seat to other activities in their busy days.

As *Signore* Big Man and his thin companion watched the commotion, some college-aged kids pulled up in an old van and quickly began to unload paperboard, banners, and even a small folding ladder they could use to mount signs on buildings and atop their van. Soon they were busily making protest signs with fat black pens. The men watched, but could not see what they were writing. No matter, they were happy with a new subject-du-jour to discuss.

They observed a black-bearded young man speaking to a girl with burgundy hair. Whatever she was writing didn't appear to suit him, and he said so. She paused, with her head bowed, as if contemplating what to do. She decided quickly, whirled around, breasts pointing and ass covered by what appeared to be painted-on jeans. The old men clearly savored the view. The girl took aim at the older boy with her breasts thrust forward like weapons; then started to yell to make her point.

The young guy shrugged, gestured "do what the hell you want" and turned away. The two old men nodded to each other their approval of her gestures, her ass and/ or those pointed breasts. Whatever their thoughts, they seemed for once to agree on an outcome. Cynthia smiled thinking men never change and regretting that her own breasts and ass didn't look that good anymore.

A growing crowd of protestors had joined the two young people. All seemed intent on their sign making and their increasingly loud conversations.

While the two men were still absorbing the drama down the street, three thirty-ish women approached. Thank God, thought Cynthia, the girls are finished shopping.

All were speaking rapid English when they entered the street from the small shoe store next door to the men. All three consulted their watches. They looked down the street and seemed alarmed by the gathering crowd of what could, God knows, be rowdy demonstrators. They turned away from the potential trouble, only to face the two old men. They waved to Cynthia and were obviously puzzled about how to get to her.

Carefully, with a giggling nervousness, they side-stepped the men, as if stepping over lazy stray dogs sleeping on the sidewalk. The men commented on the big breasts of the redhead and the interruption of their chatter, but otherwise paid no more notice of them.

"My goodness, Cynthia," said Stacy. "You'd think we could find a pair of shoes in less than forty-five minutes."

"I really am sorry we kept you waiting so long," agreed Linda. "I found the shoes I wanted right away, but then I couldn't get waited on. And of course, it's so hard to understand them. You'd think they'd learn some English. You must be dying of boredom sitting out here so long."

None of the three sat down. Debbie rested her three sacks on the table, looking at her watch again as if she expected a different answer. But only a couple of minutes had elapsed.

"Don't worry about it," Cynthia commented. "I've been enjoying resting my feet and watching the people. Besides, Roger will probably be happy I didn't spend as much money as you all did," she said observing their bulging shoe bags with a smile.

"I really think we should go now," Stacy said. "With all this talk about terrorists lately, I'm worried about that crowd down the street. Why don't we walk down to the piazza and try to find a cab."

"I'm nervous," Linda added. "And worn out. Are you ready, Cynthia?"

Cynthia really wanted to watch a little longer, but she smiled again.

"Just let me take care of my bill."

Cynthia was still intrigued by the activities on the street; the same ones that seemed to scare her companions. Maybe because they were all small-town girls, she thought. Cynthia had grown up in St. Louis where blacks and foreigners were commonplace. She sorted the Euros to pay for her drink. But she didn't hurry. She lingered as she gathered her bag and donned her jacket. Her eyes never left the men.

The growing crowd down the street began to infringe on the old men's territory. Just about the time they were starting to complain to each other they took note of an Italian woman quickly wheeling her baby through the milling students. She looked apprehensive, as the crowd grew louder and larger, closing in around her. She pushed on and emerged from the crowd unscathed except for a broken baguette of bread. She took her loss in stride, however, she didn't appear to be willing to chance another unpleasant encounter. She steered the carriage across the street to avoid the old men, thinking it safer to be on the same side as these foreign women. She passed Cynthia and her friends without looking up. Cynthia noted she wore the prerequisite yellow and brown bowling shoes and a yellow wool fringed scarf twisted and knotted around her neck. *Tres chic.*

Signore Big Man conferred with the thin man; an exciting morning, after all. It would give them much to talk about tomorrow. But for now the crowd was encroaching. Cynthia watched as the men collected their chairs and made their own exit down the street. The sky had become overcast anyway.

Hands of Dust

by Coco Tralla

In the heart of the Eternal City amid ancient fountains and cobblestone alleyways, a leather shop pokes out between tilted buildings that smell of earthen clay and weathered limestone. On the edge of the prestigious couture district, this storefront domain exhibits exquisite craftsmanship simply through its window display alone. The smell of resin mixed with wood glue from the nearby artisan's shops floats through the air and the fresh odor of tanned leather hides intoxicate those who dare venture past.

Angelo Borromeo, enticed by the smell of leather goods, entered the shop on *Via del Babuino* and dreamed of one day being able to buy his wife a pair of leather gloves from Machiavelli Leathers. He touched a butter-colored dress coat and wondered how the leather could feel as soft as a baby's behind. Now he knew why this shop in *Roma*, known for its quality skins, manufactured the finest leathers in the world. Angelo knew that the owner, Niccolò Machiavelli, maintained a reputation of providing his customers not only with genuine Italian leather but also with the most unique.

"*Buona sera.*" Niccolò's voice came from behind.

"I'm looking for gloves," Angelo said, yanking his hand away from the leather and turning around. "For my wife."

"You are the musician, the one who plays at the *Piazza Navona*, no?"

"I perform beside my wife, Allegra, she's a palmist," he said, watching Niccolò pull a soft rag from his pocket to brush the leather coat exactly where Angelo had touched it.

"A what? Never mind, I remember you," he said. "Come, see my collection in back—it's far more creative than the ones here."

As the shopkeeper headed toward the ebony curtain in the back of the store, Angelo hesitated, surprised that a person of Niccolò's wealth would bother with the likes of him. He shrugged, curious to see the man's precious leathers. Niccolò pulled the velvet curtain aside as Angelo stepped into the back room. But when Angelo passed through the opening, he felt a sharp blow to his head and collapsed to the floor.

Angelo awoke the instant he found himself immersed in a pit of fluids that kept sucking him under. Struggling to stay afloat, he realized the pit was actually a vat of churning liquids—toxic liquids. He gagged from the smell and liquid seeped into his mouth as he bobbed under. He yelled for help and grabbed onto the edge, then pulled himself up. He saw Niccolò's feet, looked up and the wicked man held a machete positioned directly above his head. The blade glistened as Niccolò held it high in the air, then dropped it to the floor. But instead of the head, Niccolò hacked off Angelo's hands.

Angelo watched in horror as his hands twitched of their own accord while he slid back into the abyss of churning toxins. Just before slipping into unconsciousness, Angelo said a final prayer, became calm and peaceful, and summoned all his senses to create an out of body experience. Angelo had practiced this many times while alive, but this time it was different because there was no turning back. After his energy field gathered and left his physical body to rise above the vat, Angelo stared in disbelief at the churning abyss below. He watched his physical body disintegrate, then looked at himself and realized his body consisted of bright blue stars. He floated in the air buoyed by the realization that he was still alive.

He swore at Niccolò standing below him, but his murderer didn't respond. At first Angelo's form swung recklessly in the air, unable to control his weightlessness, but finally he managed to lower himself to the floor. He moved close to Niccolò in an attempt to strike him, but his arm passed right through Niccolò's face. Angelo stared at the stars that composed his celestial limbs and realized he had no hands. His hands had meant everything to him. His beautiful hands had played sonatas, fugues and preludes—they were the mastermind of his existence, his creative muse. Angelo winced as he longed for his hands. He tried to mentally make them fuse back onto his arms, but the severed hands remained motionless on the floor. Bending over, Angelo wanted to weep but had no tears.

A vast hopelessness overtook him as he watched Niccolò bend down, pick up the bloody hands, then carry them to the workbench. The instant the man touched his hands, Angelo doubled over in pain. But the ache stopped when Niccolò set the hands down on the table. The shopkeeper walked back to the vat, then fell to his knees. Angelo froze when the thoughts of his own murderer became loud and clear.

Niccolò peered into the vat and wondered if this new alchemy of chemicals would decompose the fat from human skin quicker than the old formula and remove the entire skins without tearing. The process worked the same way boiling water removed skin from a potato, but this time he hoped he could pull the entire skin from the vat without sifting through the solution for remains.

The store front door chimed. Niccolò leaped up and covered the severed hands with a piece of pliant leather. Through the peephole in the curtain, he glared at a petite woman touching what he'd once considered his finest leather gloves. He frowned when her fingers caressed the leather, then turned the glove over to examine the other side. With wild raven hair and mysterious eyes, he now remembered seeing her at the *Piazza Navona* telling fortunes with the street people of the night.

"*Buona sera*," he said, slipping behind the counter to help her try on the glove. "*Lasciami aiutare*."

"Thank you," she said.

Angelo recognized that voice—it was Allegra. He floated through the black curtain and into the front of the store where he cried out to warn his wife, but she couldn't hear him.

"You speak English?" Niccolò asked, surprised a street person would be bilingual. As he helped her take the leather glove off, he ran his finger down her palm. "An English speaking palm reader?" he asked.

Her thick curls bobbed when she nodded her head. "The lines of the palm are energy lines of your unique spirit," she said, letting him touch her palm. "The imprint of each palm speaks to me because it has a message about those things we cannot change."

"What does mine say then?" He opened his hand and held it out to her.

He watched her murmur something as she studied his palm. While she traced the lines with her finger, Niccolò stared at the back of her hand admiring her flawless skin. Perfect width and length.

"You have many powers," she said. "Lines in the palm designate things that happen to you in this life. Things you don't have free will or choice about. Things that happen because it's a blueprint of the path you signed up for before you were born."

A rustling sound came from behind the black curtain.

"Excuse me, I must check on something. Please look around," he said. Thankful to leave the gypsy, he slipped behind the curtain and wondered what could have made such a sound. The hides looked as if they had moved atop the table. Niccolò yanked off the skins suspecting a nasty mouse. But underneath the leathers, he stared in disbelief at the hands. They had moved. He'd left them palms down. Now the palms were up.

"Oh my God," Allegra said. "Angelo's hands."

Niccolò grabbed the mallet from the workbench before he turned around, then in one continuous arc, struck her head and she crumpled to the floor.

When she moaned, he dropped the mallet and grabbed the machete. But just as he was about to drop the blade on her head, Allegra opened her eyes and smiled. Her complacent smile forced him to freeze, machete in the air, poised to slice her neck.

"Your palm," she said. "Don't you want to know what it said to me? There's a message."

Niccolò blinked, not wanting to listen to this wild woman, yet curious about her message.

"You are about to experience the power of death," she said, apparently unafraid and totally at peace. She closed her eyes.

Niccolò grimaced as his hand muscles grew limp and he released the machete. It crashed to the floor. He turned to run, but one glance at the severed hands made him stop. The hands had changed again from palms up to closed fists. As he moved toward the back door, the sole of his shoe caught on the blade of the machete and he tripped into the sunken vat of gurgling muck. Engulfed by the alchemy of bubbling elements, he struggled to pull himself out, but his hands wouldn't move and his muscles no longer worked. The agitating chemicals sucked him into the abyss.

Allegra rushed toward the severed hands on the worktable.

As Angelo's celestial body floated above the scene, he concentrated on making the hands move with his mind and realized he was beginning to get better at it. While he was alive, he'd used psychokinesis to move physical objects with his mind, and now that same principle seemed to work with the hands. He wanted to embrace his wife with his ethereal form, but since he'd used most of his energy to move the hands he could only sink to the floor and curl into a ball as he tried to stop the pain from his missing hands. The stumps of his arms throbbed as his wife gathered up his hands, put them into a black box and turned to leave. As Angelo's pain worsened, he instinctively said a prayer to ask for help.

At the far end of the room a presence appeared out of the darkness and Angelo's fear subsided. As if stone could transform into life, the angelic form looked exactly like the statues at the Pantheon as it moved closer until he could see every detail of the magnificent figure.

"I am Gabriel, Archangel of Birth and Death," the presence said. "I've come for Niccolò."

"Why not me?" Angelo asked, incredulous that this angel would want the killer not the victim.

"You have created this earthly reality, and now your soul must evolve before moving on."

"Evolve to where?" he asked, but the angel was too engrossed in what had emerged from the pit. Gray matter oozed up from the vat, then dissipated into thin air.

"His consciousness was not evolved enough to go to a spiritual level, so it will come back to earth as a lesser form," the androgynous angel said.

"What do you mean *lesser form*?" Angelo asked, wondering what that made him. "How am I to evolve?"

"Look to your soul for the answer." With those words, the presence disappeared.

Cringing from the dread of this hollow existence, Angelo followed closely as his wife walked to their apartment in the Ghetto. He needed her support, her love more than ever now. He was a lost soul, destined to haunt the vestiges of earth because he'd been deserted by everyone, even the Angel of Death. When Allegra arrived at the flat, Angelo's sickly form rested on the floor beside her because the journey had worsened his pain. Allegra placed the black box on the table, then positioned a picture behind it. Angelo closed his eyes as her thoughts filled the room.

Allegra scanned the flat she'd shared with her husband in marriage, and tears formed in her eyes. Paralyzed by the senseless killing and stunned by the way he died made his death even more unbearable. Everywhere she looked reminded her of Angelo and their life together. He'd died in pain. Just knowing he'd suffered in such a horrid way made Allegra ache inside. She couldn't move. She didn't even want to live anymore. But then she looked at his picture and realized she needed to remember him and carry on because that would be what he'd want her to do.

Allegra placed her hand on the black box and tried to intuit what happened to her husband in those last moments. Normally she couldn't predict what would happen to those closest to her, but she'd known something sinister happened the night Angelo died. After she'd felt his spirit leave his body, she used her intuition to guide her to Machiavelli Leathers. The minute she'd looked at Angelo's palm, the day they first met, Allegra knew his life would be shorter than most.

And now her life was a void without him near. She closed her eyes and a tear slid down her cheek. An image of Angelo's dark eyes and jet black hair surfaced in her mind and she imagined hearing his voice whisper his love. A breeze pressed against her lips as if she'd just been kissed by something that didn't exist.

The candlelight flickered when she opened her eyes. With his picture placed directly behind the box, his image evoked pure love. Allegra placed the wisteria blossoms he'd given her this morning on either side of his effigy. That morning he'd gathered the flowers from outside their balcony window, then arranged them in the jelly jars to accompany the breakfast he'd prepared. She considered the blooms an offering to honor his spirit. A multitude of candles some small, some skinny and tall, filled the empty spaces on the table so that this altar provided a remembrance, an acknowledgement of the sacred time she once had with her one and only love.

Maybe he could transcend death. Many times he'd had out of body experiences, and he'd even told her about visiting other dimensions through meditations and dreams. When he was alive he'd referred to death as a passing, a journey from one place to another, and day after day he kept telling her this life was only one of many. He called it the evolution of the soul.

She knelt at the altar, then reached out her hand, reverently brushed her fingertips over the lid, then lifted it. Goosebumps spread from her arms to her legs when she realized his hands had changed from curled digits to fingers stretched out flat, palms up.

The bloodied stumps were now totally healed over. Angelo's severed hands looked as if blood still pumped through them, and they would surely move at any moment. Beads of sweat formed on Allegra's brow as she grappled with what she should do. These hands were alive.

Slowly reaching into the box, she touched his index finger. It was warm. The fingers reached up to grab her. Allegra snapped her hand back and slammed the lid back onto the box, gasping for air. But severed hands could never be beautiful, and they can't live without a heart. She shook as she grabbed a trowel and carried the box outside. Descending the steps into the courtyard below, she kneeled down under a canopy of wisteria blooms. Stabbing the ground with the trowel, she frantically tried to avert the danger of this sinister presence. It couldn't be Angelo's spirit inside those hands; it had to be something dark using her husband's remains.

Once she'd dug the hole deep enough, she carefully placed the box inside, then pushed the dirt back into the hole until the box was totally buried under a foot of soil. Once the hands were buried, Allegra wept on her knees. Through her tears, she reminded herself to place a marker on the grave in the morning. If she kept busy with these things, maybe she could forget the ache of knowing he'd died a torturous death. At least now she could visit his grave. In time, maybe she'd even heal.

She said a prayer, then wiped her dirty palms against her tattered jeans. Ascending the stairs, Allegra gasped for breath. But when she opened the door to the apartment, she saw the hands. They gripped Angelo's picture amid a chaotic mess of spilled water and toppled wisteria blooms.

Angelo's celestial form wavered—unable to console his wife—his energy diminished by moving the hands. Angelo realized he had more power over his hands than ever before. Being able to materialize them from the grave back into the flat had surprised even himself. The pain grew, but his powers seemed to grow with that pain. His dismembered hands clutched the photo, while Allegra screamed, then covered her mouth with her hands. Angelo concentrated on making his hands place the photo where it'd been before at the center of the altar. Then he made his hands climb back into the box, placing them down in remorse as if being punished for trying to communicate.

Allegra calmed down while the hands rested in the box. And when she drew closer, he knew this time he wouldn't try holding her fingertips with his displaced ones. She moaned as she rushed to the bedroom and collapsed on the futon.

He couldn't believe she'd want to bury the only thing left alive—his most precious hands. His hands were the only things that responded to his thoughts; the only things that acknowledged his existence. And his hands were the only things that would respond to his will. He'd even made his wrists heal.

In time he knew he could attach his hands onto his celestial form, and then he'd come back to Allegra again. Come back to please her with his hands like he'd done so many times while they made love. Angelo stared at the hands that glowed with life in the box. They pulsed with energy and vibrated with life. The pain subsided when he focused on the hands, yet when he looked down, his ethereal form had changed from bright shimmering stars to a gray gauze that looked as if it would tear at any moment.

His exhilaration changed to depression in an instant and he felt the energy drain from his ethereal form as he gently lowered himself to the floor. He was dying. Just like Niccolò, he was transforming into a lesser form and soon the gray mass would dissipate into oblivion.

Sprawled on the floor, Angelo noticed a ray of light streaming through the small window of their flat. Shining on his arm, the light mesmerized Angelo because it lit up the stars in his arms, turning the gray into shades of violet, purple and azure. The light made his arm come alive with beauty, and Angelo finally realized what he needed to do. His celestial death was caused by his attachment to the physical reality he'd once known. If he could let go of his yearning to make love and touch Allegra or make music with the creative muse of his hands, then he could move from the earthly realm to the next.

As if responding to his thoughts, Gabriel appeared. "You understand now." The archangel shimmered with alabaster light and dispelled all darkness from the room.

Angelo rose up from the floor and gathered all his strength to move his right hand out of the box. He willed his hand to pick up a pencil by the phone on the table, then he wrote the words on the wall.

My Love,

For these hands to die, they must turn to dust.

As ashes, they become eternal.

He returned his hand to the box, then made his hands press against each other as if in prayer. If Allegra could help him now, then he could help her in spirit. But if his hands stayed alive, he'd remain stuck in a lesser form between the spirit world and the physical reality he once knew on earth.

Eventually, Allegra stopped crying and entered the room. The minute she walked in, she saw the note. Staring at the wall, she looked as if she understood. She hesitated, then stoked up the fireplace, turning back to look at the note again and again. Once the fire roared, Allegra surprised him. She picked up his hands, sat down and held them in her lap. She placed her hands over his as if in prayer too. Her soft hands pressed against the back of his, and she whispered his name. Angelo willed his hands to open, palms up, so that she could place her hands in his. Holding hands the same way they'd done before in marriage, he vowed to guide her in spirit for as long as she lived.

Angelo removed his right hand from Allegra's and pointed to the fireplace. She shook her head, but Angelo willed his fingertips to trace the destiny line in his palm. After a moment, she nodded and kissed first one palm, then the other. Finally she carried the severed hands to the fireplace.

"Blessed be," she said, releasing the hands into the vibrant fire.

Angelo's invisible lips formed into a smile as Gabriel came to his side.

"There is no pain in the fire of death," Gabriel said. "Ashes contain the soul, the spirit of what remains on earth forever."

As Angelo brushed Allegra's cheek with his ethereal hand, she wiped away the tears and smiled.

Memories of a Lifetime
by Marie E. Reid

It wasn't a marriage made in heaven,
Still, we thought it would never end,
Yet three years ago today I didn't lose just a husband,
or a lover,
But truly my best friend.
Our last days together were filled with hope, and pain
That left a heartrending sadness still remembered,
again and again.

Those bone-rattling hiccups, a side effect of
chemotherapy
Left your emaciated body tired and weary.
The nights I had to sleep in another room,
Your sweat reeking of deadly chemicals, an acid stench
that burned my eyes and nose.
I cried when you slept. I cried when I was alone so no
one would know.
I died a little bit inside with each day growing closer
and closer to your end.

So thin, so fragile, a shadow of your former self.
Your once buff body. . .scrawny, stomach protruding,
Flesh hanging loosely on your skeletal frame,
Your ribs etched into the skin.
A face once so handsome, now gaunt. . .sunken cheeks,

Teeth protruding like ill-fitted dentures, and dark
smudges under your eyes.
Oh. . .but those eyes. Beautiful baby-blue eyes, still so
alive, still with a spark of life.
It was macabre to see your smooth, unblemished,
caramel-colored skin,
The perfect backdrop for the startling blue clarity of
your eyes, turn sallow.
And those long, dark lashes. . .a woman should be so
lucky.

I still get that hitch in my breathing, accompanied by
the familiar tightness in my chest,
Thinking about the loss of the comfort of your arms,
When we couldn't cuddle like we used to in the morn-
ings before going off to our respective jobs.
The skin on your arms had become parchment-dry,
Scabby looking tracks of your overused veins
prominently displayed.
Caressing had become too painful.
Chemotherapy had done a job on you.

Having to settle for a feather-light kiss on your dry,
cracked lips instead,
I never missed a thing as I watched you struggle out of
bed.
I noticed your listless movements, saw your brow
furrow periodically,
The intermittent grimacing indicative of the terrible
pain you were feeling.
I knew it was a front for my benefit, acting as if you
weren't getting weaker.
And for my part, it was becoming harder and harder
not to react,
Not to reach out and comfort, not to offer assistance.

Then there was the constant loss of blood, siphoned off
by the tumor,

Making you much too sensitive to temperature change.
I remember you sitting around the house bundled up
in a sweater,
Wearing earmuffs, asleep, cocooned in a blanket.
I remember your bony legs dangling over the side of
the bed,
Your feet encased in two pairs of thick, gray and white
socks. . .
I still think of Bugs Bunny.
Our humor never wavered,
I still hear your laugh, remember your beautiful smile.

I had to leave the house each morning with the usual
trepidation,
What if you died while I was gone?
It was such a useless, monotonous ritual repeated
daily,
Because I knew I had no control over when you died.
Being there wouldn't have stopped the process.
And I couldn't stay home with you every day.
It irritated you. . .you thought I was being
over-protective,
Insisted I go on with my life.
Then I became irritated, there were the sniping
arguments,
I fell into guilt mode.
Did you know what you were asking of me?
To go on with my life. . .
Didn't you realize that *you* were my life?

I tried to carry on as usual.

As I ran my fingertips down the side of your face,
You would lean into the caress and smile,
And I would leave the house fighting back the tears.
It hit me like that, the oppressive sadness.
How arrogant we humans have become,
To think that we have the power over life and death.

It seemed like forever, since the travesty began,
But it was only two-and-a-half years. . .then just a
matter of days.
You were the healthiest person I had ever known,
Never sick a day in your life, until then.
Now thirty-three years of marriage, thirty-five years of
friendship
Has come to an end.
Oh, I knew life wasn't fair,
I was the one who had been sick from birth.
Life's little ironies. . .you were called home.

It should have been me.

When in Rome

by Susan Agee

"You look like you're lost."

The sound of English being spoken stopped Julia's progress, and she turned around to find that the words were being spoken to her. She had left her spot at the top of the Spanish Steps and pushed herself into the throng of people. She felt like the proverbial sore thumb, a sharp contrast to the mostly dark heads and skins that surrounded her. A man was whistling behind her and she couldn't place the tune. It reminded her of something from an old western movie, or maybe the music they play while game show contestants are trying to come up with that last answer that will make or break them. That tune seemed like it had been in the background of this day forever. The aroma of baking bread was present as well, and in this crowd, it was mingled with cigarette smoke.

"Are you lost?" The tall, fair man with unruly hair spoke again as he looked down at her.

"No," she said. "I'm familiar with the area by now."

He smiled at her. "Okay, then."

He started to turn away, so Julia blurted out what was on her mind. "You don't look Italian."

He turned back to her. "No, I'm not. Australian by birth, British by habit." He held out his hand. "I'm Thomas."

"Julia." Thomas held on to her hand for a moment after they shook and he studied her face.

"You're obviously not a native, either," he said. "American?"

"Yes," Julia said.

"Are you here as a tourist?"

"No, I'm studying art."

"You're an artist, then? Or just one who appreciates art?"

"I'm an aspiring artist," she said.

"Hm." Thomas nodded, then indicated an outdoor cafe across the street. "Would you like a cappuccino?" he asked.

"Yes, that would be nice."

She followed him to cross the street. "The secret is, do not hesitate," he said. As he spoke these words, his eyes were constantly keen on the traffic and at the right moment, he simply walked out into the street.

Julia followed and they worked the magic of slowing the erratically moving cars.

"I suppose you've been told to be careful of the gypsies," Thomas said as they took a seat at a table. Julia followed his eyes as he indicated a woman sitting in a doorway nearby. She was holding a toddler and had a pan for money sitting on the ground beside her. "They're not Italian, either," Thomas continued. "A lot of them are from Yugoslavia. They come here to prey on the tourists. Sometimes they break their children's limbs just to bring in more money."

Julia gasped involuntarily.

Thomas met her eyes with his own. "Yes," he said. "It's the worst kind of manipulation." They both watched as the woman whispered into the ear of the crying child.

"On a lighter note," Thomas said, "I see you brought your camera."

Julia nodded and laid the new camera on the table. "I look for scenes and people to paint," she said. "It's easier than carrying around an easel."

Thomas laughed. "Yes, I imagine it is. Have you seen the artists at work in *Piazza Navona*?"

"No."

"Oh, you must. I can take you there, after our coffee," Seeing the caution on her face, he said, "I'll bring you right back to the steps, where I found you."

Julia agreed.

A little while later, as they walked, Thomas was greeted by an Italian friend. The dark, husky young man's eyes darted from Thomas to Julia. While the two men spoke brisk Italian to each other, Julia looked at the aged buildings that rose all around them. Some of them were gray or stone colored, and some were in ice cream shades of pastels that looked like something out of a children's book. There was a feeling of busyness as clusters of shoppers and business people walked by them, and the aroma of cigarette smoke still lingered just above them in the air. After a few minutes, Julia felt Thomas's hand on her elbow and they began to move away from the young man. Before they could part, he took Julia's hand and kissed the back of it, his dark eyes gazing into hers all the while. Then suddenly, he was laughing and they were moving away from him. "*Ciao-ciao!*" he called out to Thomas.

As they walked away, Thomas bent over to check her expression. "These Italian lovers, they never let up," he said. They both laughed and Julia felt a certain comfort in moving closer to him.

They reached the *Piazza Navona* and Julia was overwhelmed at the size and the atmosphere of it. "It's like a big playground," she said, "a place where anything goes."

"I knew you'd like it," Thomas said. "Shall we look at the art?" They walked over to the nearest artist. The man smiled and exchanged a greeting with Thomas and nodded to Julia. He was taking a break, but with a wave of his hand invited them to look through his printed works. The next artist they came upon was working intently, not taking notice of anyone around him. An older woman sat next to his table with a cash box in her lap.

"The proverbial Italian mother," Thomas whispered to Julia. The old lady watched them with sharp eyes.

"I like that one," Julia said, watching the artist work. "I wonder how much he'll charge for it?"

"M'scusi?" Thomas launched into a conversation with the artist and Julia moved around the table to get a better look at his other work. When she was next to the where the woman sat, a dark hand grasped her wrist. She turned to find the sharp eyes looking directly into hers.

"Attenzione!" the woman whispered.

"M'scusi?"

The woman spoke to her in sentences that ran together and settled somewhere outside of Julia's understanding.

"I'm sorry...what..."

The old woman let go of Julia's wrist as Thomas approached them. He took hold of her other arm and pulled her a little away from the two Italians, speaking to her in muffled tones. "You have to be careful with those people. They take advantage of the language barrier. She was probably quoting you some outrageous price, just as he did with me. You do have your valuables in a money belt?"

"Yes, but I have shopping money in my pocket."

"That's fine," said Thomas, keeping his voice low.

The price of the artwork she wanted was too high, Thomas insisted, but Julia maintained that she wanted just one indulgence from her trip. She went into the ladies room of a cafe to get enough money from her belt, but slipped the change into her pocket rather than returning it to its safe place. "I need to go back now anyway," she said.

Thomas took her back to the Spanish Steps, as promised. They were still teeming with people, mostly young adults. "Our shopping malls at home serve this same purpose," Julia told Thomas, "but they're just a cheap imitation."

She heard the whistling again, the same song but this time slower, like the whistler was winding down with the day. "Do you hear that?" she asked.

Thomas nodded. "You have to be careful," he said. "You have the face of an angel, and there are devils lurking about." He kissed her once on each cheek.

"My hotel isn't a far walk from here," she said. "And it isn't really dark yet."

He nodded as he held both of her hands in his. He kissed them each and then let go. "*Ciao*," he said as he walked away.

"*Ciao*," Julia said as he walked away. But she wasn't sure if he heard her.

As she started walking in the direction of her hotel, she wondered why she hadn't given him her phone number. But I told him where I'm staying, she thought, he can find the number if he wants to.

The whistling was growing closer and Julia looked up to see the whistler standing at the top of the steps. It was the young Italian Thomas had talked to earlier and he smiled and waved at Julia. She waved back and as her arm came back down it hit the head of a small, dark boy. He looked up in surprise and grimaced, but completed his task of picking her pocket and ran off into the crowd.

"Hey!" Julia's cry was lost in the noise of the crowd. She looked up to where the whistler had been, but he was gone. Her hand went to her pocket and felt the vacancy there, then to her waist where the money belt was still attached, but empty. Julia turned around and began retracing her steps, fighting her way back through the crowd to where she and Thomas had parted.

Before she ever reached the spot, she saw him, his blond head towering above the people around him. She felt a wave of relief and began moving faster. As she drew closer to him, his unmistakable accent drifted over the din of music and voices.

"You look like you're lost."

Roman Rendezvous

by Sandra Richardson

"*Roberto,*" stated the boldly scrawled signature on the bottom of her street portrait. Amy's artistic eye admired the strong lines capturing her essence in simple broad strokes of black and white. Minimal shading of chin and cheeks added depth and definition. The street portrait was an accurate, quick capture of her clean cut, yet scruffy-edged, American cheerleader features, attributing a touch more beauty and poise than she yet possessed. The skillful artist had also easily reproduced her own slavishly sketched Bernini's Fountain of the Four Rivers, capturing the artist and her art in his own.

"Roberto's Rome". What a wonderful souvenir, Amy thought. Art for art's sake. The artist sketching the artist sketching the art of her favorite artist. Her gaze shifted from the street artist's portrait in her hand to the Roman panorama from her hotel balcony, the afternoon sun glinting on St. Peter's dome, turning the entire city into gold-washed art.

Room service arrived with her Italian coffee—a small, but mighty *macchiato*. Coffee and *gelato* were new passions to pack on her return to Colorado tomorrow. That and "Roberto's Rome."

She loved repeating his name as she sipped the strong, creamy liquid. She loved the way the "r"s wrapped around her tongue as she repeated them. She liked the feel of the "berrr" center of it, resonating deep in her chest like a cat purr. "Roberrrto," she purred the name again.

She liked his style too. The smooth way he had engaged her by offering his tattered black pashmina scarf to wipe her pastel-smudged fingers when the wind had whipped away her Kleenex. She remembered that magic moment when their hands touched, as she returned his scarf. That instant connection, a momentary spark of recognition of something meant to be, hot and jolting as an electric shock. It ended so fast that the next moment she wondered if it had been real or imagined. She remembered his casual good looks: the chin and mouth chiseled in olive flesh like the classical features of the statues she had come to Italy to study. She remembered falling into his deep blue-black eyes as they held hers, while trading the returned scarf for his sketch. She liked the fact he had noticed her, studied her, captured her. He was exactly what she had imagined in her plane flight fantasy of a Roman romance.

Her eyes drifted back to the sketch and saw with surprise something she had missed before. The faint image of a sunshine yellow tulip with a long green stem lay glowing at her feet.

That's odd, she thought, blaming the excitement of their meeting for distracting her normally keen artist's eye. Guess I'm more tired than I thought.

She headed for the shower and a good night's sleep before her long flight the next evening.

That night, Amy dreamt the same dream she had had on her field trip to Egypt. The God of Love had come to her with a golden flower, a symbol of the eternal love between them.

In the morning, Amy picked up the sketch to peruse again with her coffee, and nearly dropped the cup. Another yellow tulip now lay at her feet in the picture. And on her sketch pad, shimmering Egyptian hieroglyphs floated on the surface of the fountain's pool.

Her face looked somehow different too. More defined

and filled in, for sure, but there was something else. Something more. An indefinable element in each line gave her face a kind of glow. A glow that spoke of something. Of happiness? No, it was more than that. There was love in the picture now.

Somehow, Roberto was communicating his feelings for her through the portrait. This had become a work of art that could only have been done by a man in love with his model.

"Oh, Roberto, Roberto," she whispered, and her heart purred each time she repeated it. "Is it you? The man in my dreams?" Suddenly, she knew she had to see him one more time before she left that night.

Amy smiled at the yellow tulips, now three, and suddenly realized the drawing was his way of psychically telling her, "Yes. It's me." And a way to give her clues where she could find him again. An Egyptian obelisk stood near that fountain. He must be waiting for her there. Amy threw on her jeans and raced back to the piazza.

Skirting the fountain, Amy headed for the obelisk. A throng of people had gathered for the magic of sun through morning mist. More artists were there as well, but no Roberto.

Other street artists just shook their heads when Amy said his name and asked in bad Italian, *"Dove Roberto?"* No one seemed to know. Then, one artist smiled and gestured for her to follow. He led her toward a lone artist, sitting apart from the crowd. Her heart rose as she saw the back of his leather jacket, dark curls flirting with the collar. Her heart rose only to tumble, as the wrong Roberto turned and flashed an unmet smile.

Amy found a policeman with limited English and explained she needed to meet someone at the obelisk.

"Oh, *signorina,*" he replied, "We have thirteen *obeliska* in *Roma.* Which one do you want? The one stolen by Napoleon? The one brought on a barge by—" Amy lost the remaining history lesson as she made one last desperate dash through the crowd of artists packing up for lunch. Her heart folded into itself, as she watched them snap paint cases shut. She should be packing too, for a plane she no longer wanted to catch.

Amy raced to one obelisk, then another, and another. Each check of the sketch saw increasing numbers of yellow tulips, tokens of invisible love, mounting at her feet. And a black horse-drawn carriage with bright, shiny red wheels had appeared in the foreground.

While eating a hastily grabbed *gelato*, she watched mesmerized as the shape of a boat began to emerge on the drawing.

"Boats! Didn't the guide book say something about boats and that piazza?"

She thumbed the tattered book and read:

"Seventeenth to nineteenth century aristocracy used to flood the piazza to reenact mock sea battles of their ancestors to delight the crowds—"

He's telling me he's back at the *Piazza Navona* again! He must be there now, waiting for me, she thought. She raced back with the certainty, the surety of someone late for an appointment.

Amy stared at her reflection in the fountain. Her lonely reflection. No boats, and no Roberto in sight. Pouting didn't make her look pretty. She could feel hot tears clawing for air.

She unrolled the sketch again. At least a dozen yellow tulips now lay at her feet. The black carriage with the shiny red wheels stood empty, waiting to carry her and her prince away. The obelisk, fully formed now in the background, gave its ancient blessing to love rekindled through the ages. Two six-pointed stone stars formed a beautiful symmetry in front of Roberto's signature. And the boat had much more detail. Water shot from spouts centered in sun faces on bow and stern.

That boat! I know that boat! Bernini's Fountain of the Ugly Boat. It was berthed at the bottom of the Spanish Steps, where she had begun her research in Rome.

For once, the frightful pace of the Roman taxi didn't

bother her a bit. In fact, it seemed slow, compared to the beating of her heart.

The scorching sun hammered her back, making the climb up hundreds of steps seem like thousands. The climb this time was much more difficult than she remembered. And the masses of tourists had all decided to go in the opposite direction, jostling her and hindering her progress as they pushed down against her up. She arrived, breathless and flustered, at the top.

Artists crowded each other for studio space, captive tourists posed on cramped boxes between. Many artists, but no Roberto. Amy didn't even ask for him this time. Time was her enemy, and it was running out on her.

I've lost him, she thought, trudging back down the Spanish Steps. Her tears refracted the sunlight, blurring her vision.

Which is probably why she misjudged the third last step, narrow and uneven, with worn-away edges from years of footfalls. Having outgrown gawkiness early in life, clumsiness in her twenties came as a shock to both ego and body. Amy slid off the step and completed her descent by skidding down the last three steps unceremoniously on her bottom.

Feeling embarrassed and thoroughly disheartened, Amy stared at the ground between her sprawled legs, wishing it would open up and swallow her. Wishing for mounds of yellow tulips to magically appear. Wishing for Roberto.

Amy sat, hurt and dejected. She sat long enough to know that no one had noticed her fall. Inches from her toes, a horse passed heedlessly by, pulling an empty black carriage with shiny red wheels. Life was going on about its business, paying her no attention.

Except for one pair of eyes that met hers. Dark, blue-black eyes, glowing at her above a single yellow tulip with a long green stem, in the hands of a man named Roberto.

The Relic

by Bill Neugent

Cis Butler froze as a metallic wail echoed through the ancient Roman catacombs and yanked her back to the present. She glanced about. No one around, and the Italian chatter of the tourists had disappeared.

A distant door clanged shut.

She hastened down the narrow corridor to the intersection where the tour group was to reconvene.

Nobody, and not a sound.

Don't panic; keep calm. They wouldn't just leave someone behind, especially this tour guide, with his penetrating gaze and flecked green eyes. He'd given her that male grin and she'd returned a shy smile. He wouldn't leave her.

She turned about, disoriented. Might she have lost the meeting point? Which way had she gone after the crypt of the popes?

Silence.

"Hello?" she ventured. Earlier, she'd zoned out at Saint Cecilia's statue, lost in herself, but the tour guide returned and had to tap her arm to disrupt her introspective trance. She'd flushed at the tingle that ran along her forearm, rippling out from his touch. No, he'd surely not forget her.

"Is anybody here?" she said, tentatively, as though she'd walked into an unlocked house. "Hello?"

Faint echoes of her call returned, shadows of her

words, as if from her own past. She felt a chill. From without or within?

Cis turned to get her bearings. She stood at the intersection of four identical tunnels, each two feet wide and bordered by rock walls in which horizontal slots had been carved for graves. The galleries rose twelve graves high. In this section, the graves stood empty, the "relics" having been removed.

She floated down the path to her right, sleepwalking through a nightmare, but for the reality of her elbow scraping against red volcanic rock. The next intersection proved identical to the last. Some distance away, another intersection appeared the same. Cis inhaled the damp air and finally raised her voice to a shout. "Is anybody here?"

Still no answer but that of her own echo, asking the same question in a shrill, discordant tone. Clammy fear crept across her skin. Would she spend the night with the dead, buried alive?

The sound of ticking from behind. Cis spun to home in on the signal, heard the frequency increase, and knew instinctively what it meant: a timer about to—

Click.

The catacombs plunged into utter blackness.

"Cissy wanna play hide and seek?" said a voice in her head, a voice she hadn't heard in twelve years.

A spasm of terror surged through her. She felt for her purse and fumbled inside it as her mind slid back. Where is that light? She dropped to her knees, emptied her purse on the stone floor, felt about with desperate hands, and gasped relief as she found the light and flicked it on.

The beam angled into the lowest grave, illuminating it alone.

Cis jerked the light aside, but the frail beam blinked, wavered, and died.

"Cissy wanna play hide and seek?" returned the teasing voice.

"No," she said aloud as vertigo twisted her mind,

which spun in the oppressive blackness, with no up and no down, only a whirlpool, pulling. Her hand clung to the plastic cylinder of the light, as though only it held her above the abyss.

"My saint," she cried aloud in prayer, "help me."

The sound of her voice broke the spell. She felt her heart thumping, like the beating of a drum that warned of danger. She gripped the light, as if to squeeze life into it. Nothing. When had she last replaced the batteries? A year ago? More. Idiot.

Then, far worse than the door that closed above, she felt a door open within, deep in her chest, and a presence emerged.

An anguished moan escaped her lips, echoed in the void, and returned as the wail of a spirit.

"Save me," she whispered, "show me the way." She felt her left hand swing to assist the right and held the head of the light firm while the right hand twisted the cylinder. The beam returned, stronger than before.

She rose, fell back against the wall, and waited for her wheezing breath to calm. Focus. She turned her mind to the reality around her, down the path of the light, away from the maelstrom that churned in her gut.

Cis Butler, you're twenty-one now, get a grip. She stooped to gather the array of objects scattered on the floor and refilled her purse, starting with the collapsible umbrella, then her rosary and its reliquary cross, and her wallet, from the largest item to the smallest, one at a time, in logical order. Logic would save her. She had only to keep her head.

She stopped moving and listened. Not a sound.

Why shouldn't she keep her head? Well, for one thing, she stood thirty meters underground, surrounded by half a million graves carved into rock and connected by a dozen miles of tunnels, a labyrinth of death that had stood for almost two thousand years.

"Are you sure you'll be...okay?" her mother had

asked, with that perpetual furrow in her brow. "You should get Gina Williams to go along."

Yet Cis had to make this journey on her own, for this was not a tour but a pilgrimage. She had to renew her strength if she was to attain the standard she'd set for herself, a standard so high she felt at times she would fall.

Now, events conspired against her, as if in a test. Her obsession for cleanliness and order had been defeated by the Italian chaos that threw her schedule into disarray. With no more English-speaking tours until tomorrow, she'd squeezed into the last tour of the day with a mixed assortment of Italian tourists and found that, when you can't speak Italian, you only see what you're missing. When every family presumes you're with someone else, there's no one to notice you've been left behind. Except the tour guide, with his large hands that had felt so unexpectedly delicate when he held her elbow as she wavered atop the stairs, reluctant to descend.

She turned a corner and found herself back at the crypt of Saint Cecilia, as though guided by an inner compass. Cis lowered herself to the floor beside the prone statue and slid her hand along the stone, along the cuts on Cecilia's neck—the sword strokes that had failed to behead her, leaving her to die by loss of blood. The martyr's body, like that of her husband, remained virgin pure. When she died, her soul rose to join the angel who loved her and had sworn to kill anyone who would befoul her.

Cis removed her rosary from her purse and clasped tight the reliquary cross, with its shard of the original sword, as shared by all Daughters of Saint Cecilia. *My dear patron, tell me of death. Is not a swift end more humane? Might those who remain alive suffer more, from fear of mortal weakness? Oh, sister, give me strength.*

The scrape of gravel.

She stopped breathing.

"Cissy, where are you?" came the voice from her past.

Deep in her chest she felt it again, primal, soon unstoppable. She would scream. No, she would not. She drew a silent breath.

Another scrape.

Her grip tightened on the light. Could it be a loose display, or a rotating fan?

A distinctive rustle. Something...no, some*one*. Yet it made no sense. If someone had returned or remained behind, he would have turned on the light.

Cold logic churned up an adrenaline rush: Not if the overhead light would drown out hers.

Cis sucked in a long breath, as if she were about to submerge. Her light illuminated a path that led her way, but at the same time told her location.

The scuff of a sole, close by.

With a sigh of despair, she flicked a finger along the cylinder and allowed her beam to die. She hugged her purse to her side, stepped down the pathway, and turned the corner, her hand against the wall for orientation. The presence welled up again in her chest.

A rustle to her right. He—she knew it was a he—must have heard her direction and moved to cut her off.

Don't let this happen, warned a silent voice. She reversed and retreated, down one corridor, and another, left for a block, and then right.

Cis gasped and found herself in pain on the rock floor. Had she blacked out? She'd run into a wall, banged her head, and signaled her location, at the end of a tunnel, with no way to go but back toward her pursuer.

She listened. Her hearing reached out, strained, and detected the crunch of shoes on sandy rock, approaching the entrance of the tunnel in which she stood trapped.

Her hands crawled up the wall to her left, exploring for a way out or a place to hide. She found sandy volcanic rock and, at the height of her thigh, a horizontal rectangle of space. An empty grave. She leaned her bottom against the ledge, lifted her right leg into the narrow cavity, and coaxed the rest of her body onto the stone bed.

The walls closed in around her. The musty smell of the old cellar returned from a distant past—the cold slab of rock against her back felt like cement.

Out, just get out. She tried to turn but the stone roof held her flat. How had she squeezed in? A jolt of panic surged; air swelled into her lungs. Her expanding chest pressed her breasts against the cold roof of the grave. She felt the touch, as though a body pressed down on hers.

She would not be fouled. Her arms fought to push the body away, hands scratching against sharp rock, but the body remained. She tried to roll over, but there was no room. Her back arched. Something cold and hard pressed against her bare navel. She twisted her head to scream and felt stone grate against her lips and teeth.

The pain jarred her.

"Cecilia? Tommy?" Her mother called from the cellar stairs. "What's going on down there?"

No, Cis thought, wresting control of her mind, I'm going to beat this. Her right hand thrust into the purse still at her side and grasped about for a weapon she could use to defend herself.

She heard herself breathing, each breath ending with a hollow rasp and a squeak, like the muted cry of a baby. She inhaled, let the air out slowly, and repeated the process, until she could breathe without a sound. She closed her eyes, as if to legitimize the darkness. Maybe the whole thing had been her imagination. Maybe the noises were natural, like the creaks in her mother's house, like—

A rustle nearby. Her eyes popped open, with no change in the view. A blinding flash exploded before her, a huge light, blasting into her eyes. She shut her eyes to save them. Her left arm flailed out. She fought to escape and rammed her left leg out the opening.

Strong hands grasped her left wrist and ankle, overpowered her struggling, and held her in place. "Hold on," he said, "I'll help you down. Sorry about the joke."

Her mind put a face to the voice: the tour guide,

who'd taken her aside and said in perfect English, "You can explore on your own; we gather here in ten minutes."

A hand under her leg, on her shoulder, the cellar floor beneath her back.

"Cissy, I found you."

"No, Tommy, please."

His hand around her waist, pulling her sideways. She heard words that made no sense. "...lifetime experience...no other tourist can say..."

It was happening again, but Cissy was ready.

His hand reached under her left leg, pulling it toward him, away from her right leg. Disembodied words. "...give you a private tour...other groups don't get to see."

She felt her body being lifted into the open, where everything she had to defend would lay before him, exposed, vulnerable. But she wouldn't be vulnerable, not while both his arms were beneath her.

As her body moved, her right hand slid out of her purse and pressed a button on the metal object she'd found. She heard a click as the blade set. When her right arm came free of the grave, she turned, gave a shattering howl, launched herself in fierce attack, and hammered the knife into the guide's chest.

"Cissy, what are you doing? Cissy!"

Warm liquid spurted down her arm and over her torso, so close to his. They fell to the cellar floor.

"Stop!" he cried, his voice already fading. "I wasn't going to—" But the knife found his groin, and found it again, and again, and again.

Cecilia knelt before the body, held high the blade with both hands, and moved the bloody weapon in the sign of the cross. *"In nomine Patris, et Filii, et Spiritus Sancti,"* spoke the voice of her angel.

Finally she rose, stepped beyond the pool of blood, retrieved the reliquary chain from her purse, shut her eyes, and said her rosary.

Cis Butler jolted alert and felt her body drenched. She glanced down at the sticky rosary in her hands, but something caught her peripheral vision. She turned toward the sprawled body, stared at it for a long breath, and for the second time in her life felt worthy to be a Daughter of Saint Cecilia.

The Portrait

by **Brian Moreland**

Rinaldi ran down the narrow alley, hugging a wrapped canvas against his chest. His heart beat wildly. His face, a clown's mask of tension, couldn't shake his giddy smile. His heels clicked along the cobblestones, stirring up a flock of pigeons. Rinaldi danced through the fluttering feather storm, howling as the birds took flight. High above, church bells chimed. Sunshine painted the sky in Van Gogh swirls of white, gold, and indigo blue. Today he would proclaim his love for Sophia Costanza, the most beautiful woman in all of Rome.

Rinaldi stepped through an archway into a courtyard with a Mercedes and Rolls Royce. He reached a massive green door, grasped the lion-head knocker and rapped three quick hollow knocks. He stepped back, shifting his weight from one foot to the other. He wiped his sweat-greased palms through his long black hair, adjusted the collar of his cleanest shirt, and cleared his throat. Having never been inside Sophia's home, he imagined the interior was like a palace, an exotic reflection of her family's wealth and power. Each day Rinaldi was amazed such a high-class girl could fall for a poor gypsy artist like himself. But she loved him, and that was all that mattered.

The large green door opened on barking hinges. A pocked-faced giant in an Armani suit stepped out. His black hair was pulled back in a tight ponytail. He looked down, eyeing Rinaldi suspiciously. "What do you want?"

"*Buon giorno*," Rinaldi grinned. "I'm here to see Don Federico Costanza. I need to talk with him, *por favore*."

The giant's pocked granite face tightened into a thin-lipped frown. "Who sent you?"

"No one. He should be expecting me."

The tall man looked around the courtyard, said, "*Uno minuto*," and shut the door.

Rinaldi stared up at the two-story windows as he waited. Sophia was probably up there somewhere. He wished she'd open a window and blow him a kiss. Or better yet, greet him at the door.

The front door flung open again, startling him.

The giant with the ponytail waved his hand inward. "Come. Federico will see you."

Holding the large wrapped canvas to his chest, Rinaldi followed the Armani giant up a winding staircase where oil portraits of old Italian men lined the walls. They entered a library with mahogany shelves embedded with hardbound books. A grand piano sat off to one corner beside a nude sculpture of a woman missing two arms. Chairs with red cushions and gold tassels sat empty on a Persian rug. A fire burned in a grand marble hearth.

"Wait here," the giant said and left the study.

Rinaldi walked over to the fireplace, staring at the huge painting above the mantle. It was the first portrait Rinaldi had painted of Sophia. He winced, seeing all the flaws in his strokes, the drab colors, the misuse of light and shadows. Her posture was traditional, proper, lady-like, and way too stiff, exactly what her mother had requested. Rinaldi had spent five hours alone with Sophia, struggling to capture her pent-up beauty on canvas. She wore a black dress with buttons to the throat and red roses on the long lacy sleeves. Her dark hair with highlights of midnight blue had been pinned up, until Rinaldi brushed the hair above her ear and a few rebellious strands sprung free and curled around her oval face. Her full lips partially opened then, a straight even mouth allowing just a hint of a smile. Her deep, chestnut brown eyes, soft and alluring, had stared right into his soul the rest of the afternoon.

Now gazing at the oil canvas, Rinaldi spotted the flaw around the buttons in her dress where his painting had come apart. He recalled her delicate fingers unfastening the buttons around her neck as he painted in a frenzy. Sophia's pinned up hair came undone and fell to her shoulders as the V of her neckline grew wider, exposing the swell of soft olive flesh beneath. He could still feel the heat of her breath on his neck, as Rinaldi unfastened the rest of the buttons and kissed her lips feverishly. The passion that had scorched his studio that golden afternoon filled the following days and nights with a burning desire to be with her every waking second.

Since then Rinaldi and Sophia had stolen moments together, meeting at cafes, the market square, or in cathedrals. Sometimes she posed nude for him back at his studio, reading him sonnets from Shakespeare, while Rinaldi stroked her delicate curves onto canvas. The affair had spanned several months, and his paintings had come to life with brighter colors and smoother strokes until she became a radiant angel with glowing auras.

Three sleepless nights had passed since their last tango between his sheets. In between warm kisses, they had talked of getting married. Rinaldi's heart tingled with joy. Soon Sophia would no longer be just a collection of portraits in his loft, but an inspiration to wake up with every day of his life.

Now, Rinaldi had only to win the heart of her family. A challenge that none of Sophia's previous lovers had overcome, for her father, Don Federico Costanza, was head of the Roman mafia.

"You have some business with me, young man," a deep voice said from behind.

Rinaldi spun around.

Don Federico Costanza had entered the study with two Great Danes, one on either side. Behind him, three men in dark suits leaned against the wall and folded their arms. Rinaldi recognized the giant with the ponytail and the Armani suit. Beside him stood a heavy set goon with no neck, and a short ferret-faced man wearing a fedora. All three glared with narrowed eyes, sizing him up.

Rinaldi's throat went dry as he looked into Don Federico Costanza's hard brown eyes. "Uh, *si, signore,* I, uh—have something very important to discuss with you."

Federico grunted and motioned to an empty red Persian chair then took a seat opposite. He was a thicker man than Rinaldi had envisioned, with a bald crown and tufts of white hair above his ears. His handlebar mustache curled in loops over a plump bottom lip. He wore a red and black smoking jacket and carried a pipe that scented the room with tobacco smoke. The Great Danes lay on either side of his chair, licking their chops. One dog growled and displayed sharp teeth. Federico patted its furrowed head. "Easy, Brutus." He looked up at Rinaldi. "So, what is it you need, young man? A loan to pay off some gambling debts? Or perhaps you have a problem with the police you'd like to go away."

Rinaldi shook his head, confused. "No, none of that. I know we've never met, but..."

Behind Federico, Sophia came down the winding stairs, her manicured hand gliding along the brass rail. Her long raven hair draped her shoulders, curls springing with each step. She wore a red silk blouse, the top two buttons unfastened, and black slacks that hugged her curvy hips. Her chestnut brown eyes widened when she saw Rinaldi.

He gazed at her, mesmerized by her beauty. Seeing her again made his heart beat faster. Rinaldi smiled and nodded to her.

The heavy set giant with no neck popped his knuckles.

Sophia froze at the foot of the stairway and looked at the three frowning goons.

Federico twisted in his chair and smiled at his daughter. "*Mi dolcia,* we're discussing business in here. Go see what your mother is doing."

Rinaldi cleared his throat. "Uh, actually, *signore,* is it okay that Sophia is present? We have something to discuss with you."

Federico twisted back around, lifting a bushy white eyebrow. "Oh? You are an acquaintance of my Sophia?"

Her wide brown eyes stared at Rinaldi. She shook her head slightly. A warning.

The gypsy blinked. Hadn't she told her father about him? He thought quickly, then offered his most charming smile to Federico. "*Sí.* I'm Rinaldi Sorgente, the artist your wife hired to paint Sophia's portrait." He pointed to the giant framed canvas above the mantle.

Federico tilted his head up toward the painting and beamed with a father's pride. "That was you?" His bottom lip curled. "Impressive. You captured my Sophia well that day. So it is payment you come for. How much do I owe you, young man?" He snapped his fingers, and the Armani giant with the ponytail pulled out a wad of cash.

Rinaldi held up his hands. "No, no, it's okay. Your wife already paid me. Didn't Sophia tell you my reason for coming today?"

Federico pulled the pipe from his lips, frowning. "No. Should she have?" The Mafioso looked up at his daughter, who had remained on the stairway. "*Dolcia,* is there something you're not telling your Papá?"

Sophia looked up, cheeks blushing, eyes wide, like a child caught in a lie. She chewed her lip but didn't answer.

Rinaldi's jaw dropped. He couldn't believe she had never mentioned him. He stared at her, confused about what he should do.

Watching the silent exchange between Sophia and Rinaldi, Federico glared at the gypsy artist with a flash of realization in his eyes. "Oh, I see." His knuckles tightened on the armrest of his chair. "Do you wish to enlighten me as to what this visit is about?"

Rinaldi fidgeted in his seat as Federico's entourage of goons and Great Danes glared with intense eyes. Rinaldi was stunned that Sophia, after so many romantic promises in the afterglow of making love, now remained meek and quiet in her father's presence. Was she ashamed of him? Rinaldi considered his options. Lie or tell the truth? Be a man or be a coward? One choice risked his life, the other his heart. But the fire in his chest was so immense, he couldn't imagine his life without Sophia. She loved him and he her. They were meant to be together.

Rinaldi sat straight in his seat. *"Signore,* what Sophia and I wanted to share with you was that...over the past several months, we've done several more portraits, and..." Rinaldi looked at Sophia, feeling tremors in his cheeks. "I've fallen deeply in love with your daughter."

Federico pulled the pipe from his lips. "You what?"

Rinaldi said, "Sophia and I are in love and—" he pushed out his chest, "with your blessing, I wish to marry your daughter."

The goons behind Federico chuckled.

The Mafioso held up his palm and they stopped. Federico's tan face turned crimson. Thick eyebrows knitted over hard brown eyes. "Absolutely not." He leaned forward, jabbing his finger at the air in front of Rinaldi. "Now you listen here, young man. I don't know who you think you're trying to swindle here, but my Sophia has never mentioned being in love with anyone, especially not a long-haired gypsy like yourself. And before you test my patience, which is about as short as your little finger, I suggest you leave and stay clear away from here."

Rinaldi's chest sank. A chill waved through him. He looked into the faces who saw him as nothing but a worthless gypsy. The filth of the city. He had been a fool to believe that a family such as this could ever accept a starving artist. He felt tears clouding his eyes, but held them in. *"Signore,* I know this is a surprise, but if you'll just get to know me. I'm a hardworking painter and a devout Catholic. I want only the best for Sophia."

"What's *best* is you staying a hundred miles away from my daughter." Federico stood, the Great Danes rising with him. "Guido, give our artist a ride home."

Butterflies of fear fluttered inside Rinaldi's stomach. "That's okay. I can walk."

"I insist," Federico motioned his hand.

The Armani giant stepped behind Rinaldi. A large hand painfully squeezed his shoulder.

"Wait, Papá, don't take him away!" Sophia said, coming off the staircase.

Rinaldi whirled around, feeling the butterflies swarming up to his chest.

Sophia ran to Federico and tugged his arm. "Please let Rinaldi stay, Papá."

Federico's jaw tightened. "*Dolcia*, stay out of this."

Her face hardened like her father's. "No, I won't. I'm tired of you deciding who I can and can't date. Rinaldi's right. I'm in love and want to marry him."

"Don't talk nonsense, Sophia. He is nothing but a gypsy. He's probably after our money."

"He's not, Papá. Rinaldi has a studio and paints the most beautiful paintings. He is a gentleman and treats me like a princess. And he loves me as much as I love him. Mother likes him, too."

Federico said, "She knows about this?"

"*Sí*, Papá. I wanted to tell you, but I was afraid you'd hurt him. I don't want you to chase him away like the others." She took Rinaldi's hand. "Please, give him a chance. I love Rinaldi with all my heart."

Federico shook his head. "I will not have my daughter marry a street artist." He turned to Rinaldi. "Okay, let's just get down to business. You gypsies all have your price. How much do you want to walk away and forget this whole thing? Five thousand Euro? Ten thousand?"

Rinaldi frowned. He may have been born from poor gypsies, but he still had his pride. He raised his chin.

"I'm not after your family's money, *signore*. And I'm insulted that you would think so. I just wanted to express how much I love your daughter and become a part of your family. But I see that's not possible. So if you'll at least honor me with the dignity of walking out of here on my own, I'll leave."

Federico remained stunned for several seconds, and Rinaldi wondered if he'd just bought himself a pair of cement boots and a one-way ticket to the bottom of the Tevere river.

The Mafioso said, "Guido, let him go."

The squeezing fingers released Rinaldi's shoulder.

Federico motioned his hand toward the exit. "You're free to leave."

Tears watered Sophia's eyes. "No, Papá."

"It's for the best, *dolcia*."

She looked to Rinaldi.

"No, you're father's right," he said, keeping his voice even. "It's best I go. But, *Signore* Costanza, please accept this as a gift." He handed his wrapped canvas to Federico. "It's the last portrait I did of Sophia. It is our gift to you and her mother."

Don Federico, glaring at Rinaldi, unwrapped the tattered cloth and pulled out the canvas. The aura of the paints seemed to glow on the Mafioso's face in lavenders, pinks, yellows, and ethereal whites as he stared at Sophia wearing a wedding gown. In the painting, her chestnut brown eyes glowed like a woman in love, her whole face smiling. Her long dark hair draped her shoulders.

Federico's hard eyes softened as they stayed locked onto the painting for several seconds. The muscles in his cheeks relaxed, the handlebar mustache dropped as he released a breath. "Dear God, Sophia…"

The room remained silent except for the crackling fire in the hearth. The three goons looked over the Mafioso's shoulder, admiring the painting. Federico showed it to them, his face beaming.

"Not bad," the goon with no neck said.

"I like how her hair glitters with sequins of sunlight," said Ferret Face.

"Yeah, this would look good in the sun room," Guido offered.

Sophia smiled, mascara running down her cheeks. "Do you like it, Papá?"

"I've never seen you look this way. It's beautiful." Finally, Federico looked over at Rinaldi. "You have an eye for detail. Do you truly love my daughter this much?"

Rinaldi nodded, heart pounding. "*Sí, signore*. More than life itself."

Federico, standing between his Great Danes, looked up at the ceiling and bit down on his pipe. Then, after a long moment, the Mafioso exhaled and stared at the young couple. "My Sophia means the world to me. I will not have her marry an artist who scrapes by for a living. But... I have a business associate who owns several restaurants in Rome and Florence. He needs an artist to paint murals. I could arrange a steady job for you, if you're interested."

Rinaldi smiled. "*Sí, signore*. I would be honored. I'll work hard. I promise."

Sophia said, "Oh thank you, Papá."

Federico nodded. "You two do not have my blessing just yet. A father's trust has to be earned over time." He motioned to the Armani giant. "Guido, go tell the cook to set another plate on the table. It appears we'll be having a guest for dinner."

Feeling butterflies swirling around his heart, Rinaldi squeezed Sophia's hand. Perhaps there was hope for poor gypsies after all.

The King of Sea Isle
by Jack Smith

"I was born without tear ducts. I'm a *sensitive* guy, but I just can't cry." At least that's what we always told the ladies. I found out several years later that it wasn't that I didn't have tear ducts; I just never had a good enough reason to use them. Until I found out about Patrick. Patrick Quigley was the King of Sea Isle, a Jersey shore town that he ruled for four glorious summers in the 1980's. We used to lift weights together and when I first asked him to take a share of our beach house I thought that I was taking him under *my* wing.

My four brothers and I are all easy-going sorts and Patrick was the same, always quick with a joke or a smile or laughter. And Patrick fit right in, like he belonged, like he was just another *brother*. And then on September 11, Patrick boarded United Flight 175 and *disappeared*.

At the time I didn't even know he was on the flight. I was at work in Golden, Colorado. It was only 6:30 AM and I was surfing the Internet when the first news story about the World Trade Center flashed across my computer screen. I had a sinking feeling in my stomach. My brother Jeff works in Manhattan. His office was just down the street from the twin towers. They seemed to be parked right outside his office window. After several minutes of frantic dialing I caught him on his cell phone, and I let out a huge sigh of relief. And then the second plane struck the South Tower.

Jeff could see the whole thing from his office window. He tried to describe the horror of it, but words failed him and I was left to listen to the anguished cries of his coworkers. It wasn't until November that my brother Greg called me with the news. He only had to say six words to make me realize that I *could* cry.

"*Patrick* was on the second plane."

On Friday nights, after our ritual dinner at Luicci's restaurant, we used to sit on the balcony of our beach house. On one night in particular, we'd had just polished off a big meal of anti-pasta, mozzarella sticks, and linguini and clams. We were relaxing, letting the meal settle before we hit the stretch of bars along the beach, just sipping ice-cold long necks and watching the sleepy shore town wake from its five-day slumber. A steady stream of autos passed beneath us. Seagulls scattered in front of the cars, then occasionally one would swoop between the fenders to grab some fallen treat. Jeeps, convertibles, pick-up trucks and the small cars favored by young ladies just out of college all rolled into Sea Isle. One right after the other, a never ending stream, and the only thing they had in common was the look of joy and anticipation on the faces of the occupants. The week was over. It was time to have some *fun*. We sat sipping our beers and watching.

"Were you guys really robbed?" Patrick asked.

"Huh?" I knew what he was asking. I just didn't know *why*. I was always impressed by Patrick. He was extremely smart, had a great job working with computers, and had been an art major in college. I was an ex-college football player turned night school accountant with the dream of being a writer. He *knew* about all about the world, while I only knew about football, lifting weights, and farming in Michigan. He was curious about *our lives*. About what it was like to grow up in a big family, in small town in rural Michigan where we slaughtered pigs inside of our high school, and our science classes had names like "Crops and Soils" and "Animal Husbandry."

That night, while the cars passed below, I knew what he was asking about. My brother Greg and I had worked at a truck stop while we were in high school. One night, after we closed, two men jumped us with sawed off shotguns. They tied us up and made us beg for our lives before they finally left. Greg must have told Patrick about it.

"Were you scared?" he asked.

I nodded. "I was scared something would happen to Greg."

"You weren't afraid of dying?"

"I was more afraid of my brother dying. But what really bothered me, was that I could tell that Greg was more afraid that something would happen to *me*."

"That must be really cool."

"What's that?"

"To have so many brothers."

"My dad used to tell Greg and I that we were responsible for looking out for everyone. Our *sisters* and our *brothers*. And we did."

"I have a sister. She's really cool. Plus, we're good friends. But it must be different having brothers." I should have told him that we all thought of him as a *brother*, but I never did. And he asked me what happened next.

"What do you mean?"

"Big Greg told me you popped some guy one night."

"Yeah. A couple of years later. I was still working at the truck stop, trying to earn money for college. This guy came in one night and tried to rip us off. So I punched him."

"You what?"

"I clocked him."

"You're kidding? You Smith brothers are animals. What happened next?"

"The police came. They were going to arrest me, and then the sheriff's department arrived. We knew all of the deputies because we handled their wrecker calls, so they got involved."

"Did they arrest you?"

"No. They ran a check on the guy. He was out on bail for *armed robbery*. They arrested *him*."

You could tell Pat was floored by the whole thing. He had graduated from Rutgers and was used to going to art museums, reading GQ, and dressing nice for work. He probably could have been a model if he'd wanted. But my brothers and I had worked on farms and in truck stops and auto-body shops and gyms and gone to night school. And I think we intrigued him.

"Why? Why did you hit him? You couldn't have cared about the money. You took a huge risk."

"When he reached inside his coat, I thought he was grabbing a gun, and I thought about *that* night. About those two men with sawed off shotguns, and how they'd threatened to kill *my brother*."

"Did you think about that when you hit him?"

"Yeah. *Each* time."

One of the realities about foreign countries is that it's easy to disappear. I'm not talking about Canada or England; I'm talking about *real* foreign countries, like Italy or Brazil, where they don't speak English. I experienced that on my recent trip to Italy. I wanted a few days to explore on my own, so I arrived in Rome ahead of my writing group. For the first time in several months, I was alone. I found that because of my complete lack of foreign language skills, every time I ventured out on the streets I felt that if I weren't careful, I could *disappear*. Because I can't understand or speak even basic Italian it was easy to be alone surrounded by people. That can be a good thing, unless you are trying hard not to remember something. Being alone in a foreign country gives you time to reflect on things.

The events of September 11th, and the long delay in finding out about Patrick's death, made the whole event seem even more surreal. I'd done a pretty good job of locking his death away, of not thinking about it, his wife Patti, his six-year old daughter Rachel, or the baby girl he'd never get to hold in his arms.

The hotel where I stayed offers an hourly shuttle bus to the popular plazas in Rome. Only a few other tourists were on board. Before we left, the driver made an announcement. He spoke to us in heavily accented English. I won't try and replicate it, but the gist was that there was a problem. Two million people were heading into the city to strike and protest. They had blocked off the bridges and the only access was via the subway. The driver told us that he could drop us off at the subway station, but he couldn't guarantee us a ride back to the hotel, or even our safety. I decided to go back to my room. On the way down the aisle, I asked him what the people were protesting.

"The United States. And their actions against the terrorists."

I sat back down.

Later that night, I was alone, seated in a small restaurant and thinking about what had happened to Patrick. I just stopped in for pizza but the owner and the waiter took turns serving me heaping portions of antipasto and about six other courses. I couldn't speak the language and I couldn't help but think of Friday nights at Luicci's and I wished Patrick were *here*.

The trip downtown hadn't brought any relief. I didn't see any terrorists. I'd hoped to find some, maybe that would help with the pain, someone that would give me the *opportunity* to feel better. But there weren't any terrorists. All I saw were tired old men and women, and kids without much of a future. They were the store clerks, bank tellers, cab drivers, mechanics and hotel doormen. They were well behaved and *polite*.

I was left to *think*. I would never be able to even this score. I'm used to fixing things, but I would never be able to fix *this*. Like that night at the truck stop, I felt helpless.

The waiter and the owner seemed to sense my pain. They constantly stopped by my table, poured wine and encouraged me to eat. I thought of Patrick. I imagined him at the table and for the first time that day, I smiled. Patrick would have been able to finish *all* of the food, and the owner would have put his picture on the wall, right next to Jennifer Capriati. That's the kind of effect he had on people.

After finishing my meal, the waiter poured shots of *grappa*. The owner made a toast but I couldn't understand him. Besides, my mind was preoccupied. I looked at my two new friends, and I realized *this* is what Patrick would have wanted. I poured three shots of the strong *grappa*.

"To *my brother*, the King of Sea Isle."

Venus Faded

by Suzanne Tyrpak

Mariana wrapped her cloak around her shoulders, raising the hood against the evening's chill. She gazed into the fountain, and the wide eyes of a girl gazed back. As she drew her fingertips through the quivering reflection, chiseled cherubs watched her from above.

Meet me tonight, Antonio had said. *Tonight, my love, we'll leave this place.* She touched the necklace he had given her. *Pray for me,* he'd said.

Closing her eyes, she felt the lingering warmth of his embrace. Within the sanctuary of his arms the world seemed good; the world seemed safe.

Church bells chimed, announcing Vespers. Mariana glanced around the empty square. Light withdrew, and inky shadows stained the cobblestones.

Where was Antonio?

Despite layers of skirts and petticoats, damp shivered her bones.

She stirred the fountain's pool—within the swirling water the image of a wizened face appeared. An old woman stared at her.

"*Buona sera, signorina,*" the old woman croaked.

"*Buona sera, nonna,*" Mariana murmured, averting her eyes.

The woman's poverty was palpable. Stoop-backed, she carried a basket on her arm. Beneath tattered skirts, her ankles were wrapped in filthy rags, and yet, Mariana noticed, a golden cross lay nestled at her throat—it sparkled in the dying light.

"*Una rosa, signorina?*" The woman reached into her basket and withdrew a blood-red rose. She offered a toothless grin.

"*No, grazie.*" Mariana shook her head. "Not tonight."

The woman's rheumy eyes gleamed within her grizzled face. "So beautiful. So proud." She stroked the velvet petals of the rose. "So delicate this life." Suddenly she thrust the bloom at Mariana. "Tomorrow will be too late."

The blossom's thorns pricked Mariana's palms. She sucked at salty beads of blood. The woman frightened her. She seemed strangely familiar, but surely, Mariana told herself, they had never met. Was she a gypsy? A half-starved beggar or a thief? Hoping to appease a pang of guilt, she produced coins from her leather pouch.

"Keep your silver," the old woman said. She smiled beatifically.

"Who are you? What is it you want?" Mariana drew her cloak in tight. Beneath its shield, she crossed herself.

The woman's eyes sharpened into fiery points. "Pray," she rasped. "Pray for your eternal soul. Pray for Antonio."

"Antonio?" Mariana's heart began to race. "What do you know of him?"

The woman worked her withered lips. Resettling her basket, she turned to go.

"Wait." Mariana caught her by the arm. "What of Antonio?"

"Take care, Mariana. Rome's streets are dangerous."

Mariana froze.

The woman limped across the square and disappeared into an alleyway. Still pondering her words, Mariana listened to her footsteps fade.

Pray for Antonio.

Something was wrong. There was something she

should see, something she should know. Shadows played over her memory.

Crushing the rose against her breast, she breathed its scent—sweet as her Antonio. She peered up at the darkening sky and Venus winked through twilight's veil.

Had he forgotten her? Had he changed his mind? She bit her trembling lip, refusing tears.

Church bells echoed up the stuccoed walls, reverberating through the little square.

Could she have been mistaken? Had he meant to meet her somewhere else? Perhaps by the river where they often stole a kiss.

One by one, she pulled the petals from the rose. *He loves me. He loves me not. Cara,* he had said, *I cannot live without you.* She sent the petals swirling in the fountain, each a tiny boat in search of love.

She pressed her palms against her swelling womb. The old hag would not frighten her. *"Caro,"* she said softly, "your papa will be coming soon."

Moonlight touched the cobblestones. Mariana blew into her palms to warm her fingers.

How dare he leave her waiting all alone? If she'd had somewhere to go, she would have gone.

Pray for Antonio.

What if he were hurt? Unable to come to her? Berating herself for allowing the old woman to escape, she gathered up her skirts and ran across the square.

Her heart beat wildly as she turned into the alleyway. She hurried by closed doors. Vacant windows watched her pass. Garbage spewed into the narrow passage, and the scent of cooking mingled with decay.

The cobbled street was slick. A cat bolted in front of her, flashing yellow eyes. Thinking she heard footsteps, Mariana glanced over her shoulder and slipped on rotten oranges. The old woman was right. Rome's streets were dangerous.

Regaining her balance, she wiped debris from her bedraggled petticoats. She paused when she heard footsteps up ahead—the shuffling gait of an old woman. Mariana hurried after her.

The footsteps led her through a maze of streets. She came to a thoroughfare which ran along the river. A carriage careened toward her, and she jumped out of its way.

Fog blanketed the shore. Beggars wandered through the rising mist. Along the river ghostly sycamores reached sylvan limbs toward heaven's face.

A young man stood upon the bridge gazing at the water. Moonlight glinted silver on his curls.

"Antonio," Mariana called.

He looked up as she approached. *Caro,* she meant to say, but her voice caught in her throat. Lines etched his face; his once full lips now sagged. Vacantly, the stranger stared at her.

Stifling a scream, she ran from the river away from the old man. Away from time. Pain stabbed her chest. Sweat left her shivering. Pausing to catch her breath, her stomach roiled.

Once more, she heard the footsteps up ahead.

She followed them along an unfamiliar street. From the rooftop of a church, a dark cross beckoned her. The church stood within a black wrought iron fence. The gate creaked on its hinges, opening.

She slipped inside the churchyard and looked up at the towering doors. From above the entryway, winged skulls glared at her. She climbed the steps leading to the doors. Lifting the brass ring, she let it fall—it answered with a heavy thud.

The doors inched open, and the old woman's face appeared. "Come in, my dear." She opened the doors a little wider.

Mariana strained to see inside, but darkness swallowed up the light. Her knees felt weak. Summoning her strength, she said with a shaking voice, "I would see Antonio."

Above the doors the skulls glittered with a sickly light. Shifting their wings uneasily, smoke issued from between their gaping teeth. Sparks shot from the sockets of their eyes.

"He waits for you inside," they hissed. "But you must offer sacrifice."

Within her womb the baby kicked. "No!" Mariana cried. As she turned to flee, the stone steps caught her boot and sent her tumbling.

"Too late," the old woman shrieked. The doors slammed shut, reverberating hollowly.

Pain ripped through Mariana, tearing the life from her, uprooting her very soul as blood coursed down her legs.

Lost within her shattered hopes, she thought she heard Antonio, "Come, my love," he called.

The skulls yawned. Within their empty eyes, smoldering coals burst into flame. "Too late," they cried. Wreaths of fire crowned their bony brows, and fiery tongues licked at their jaws. Extending hideous wings, the skulls flew from the walls and lashed at Mariana, scorching her.

Blinded by tears and driven by an instinct to survive, Mariana crawled out of their reach.

They followed her.

"Antonio is dead!" they howled.

Clinging to the iron fence, she hoisted herself up and flung herself against the gate. It swung wide, expelling her into the gutter of the street.

Her head hit stone and darkness overtook the light.

She woke within a pool of blood, soaked skirts strangling her thighs. Cradling her womb, she felt the stillness of her unborn child. She could not move. She had no will to breathe. Despite dawn's brightening sky, she saw no light.

A carriage whipped around the curb, spraying her with water. Forcing herself to rise, she gathered her tattered skirts and struggled to her feet. She wandered aimlessly.

There was no time. There was no child. There was no Antonio.

As church bells ushered in the day, Mariana found herself again beside the fountain.

Scooping handfuls of cold water, she washed away salt tears. As she bent over the fountain's pool, a wavering reflection gave her pause: the old woman gazed back at her. Within the water's depths, blood-red petals drowned.

Stooping painfully, Mariana placed her basket on her arm. She squinted at the sky where Venus faded with the light.

Whispering a prayer, she touched the golden cross she always wore—a gift from Antonio.

"Una rosa, signorina?" she called out to a passing girl.

"No, grazie, nonna. Not today."

Church bells rang, and chiseled cherubs watched as Mariana hobbled through the square.

The Photographer
by Olivia Barbee

"*Piazza Navona,*" the tour guide said through his handheld microphone. "Everybody out."

Walter's white-haired fellow tourists lined up and shuffled slowly off the bus. They kept close together as they moved, clutching tight their purses and camera bags—for everyone knew that Rome was a den of pickpockets—and filling the air with their craven chatter.

"Do you think there are more pickpockets here than at the Trevi fountain?" they said to each other. "I should have brought gloves; there's a nip in the air. And do you think there's a leather shop in the piazza? I would hate to have to travel too far for leather."

Walter found himself trapped behind the most-active complainers, two elderly Alabama sisters who in the midst of their nonstop whine seemed determined to walk only five steps before stopping and searching about their persons for a misplaced piece of paper or an old cough drop. *Dorothy would get a kick out of these two. They're fussy just like her Aunt Alice,* Walter thought as the trio continued their slow progress. He pulled out his camera and turned off the flash. Click. A surreptitious picture of the sisters in mid-complaint.

At last the group exited into Rome's cold morning. Walter buttoned his jacket against the wind and followed the guide across a chaotic street into the piazza. They stopped in front of a white stone fountain featuring several half-clothed women surrounding a muscular nude man. The guide began to talk about the piazza, the fountain, and myriad other things in which Walter had no interest.

The piazza seemed to him nothing more than a large cobblestoned oval filled with peddlers and fountains and ringed by shops. Nothing worth getting on a plane for, surely. He could find shops and fountains back home in Minnesota. Peddlers, too. He was only here because of Dorothy. She'd wanted to visit Rome for at least ten years. Talked about it all the time.

Walter raised his camera and aimed at the white stone fountain. Click, click, click. Three pictures of the fountain. He walked around to the opposite side. Click, click. Another two. Dorothy would be pleased.

The guide was still talking. Walter yawned and checked his watch. He had a good twenty minutes before the tour bus departed for its next stop and he hadn't taken nearly enough pictures. He edged away from the group and ambled toward the middle of the piazza, camera at the ready. A dark-skinned young sunglasses peddler approached and, through sign language, tried to tempt Walter into buying a cheap-looking pair of glasses with a burgundy frame. Click, click. One of the peddler and one of his tray of sunglasses. Behind the peddler, a short, squat, black-sweatered old woman struggled to contain her three excitable miniature white poodles. Click. One of the old woman and the poodles.

In front of him, Walter saw another fountain with more nude people. What was it with Italians and undressed statues? He'd toured Rome for three days now and had yet to meet anyone walking outside without clothing. Odd that they'd want to see that in their art. But he knew nothing of such matters. Dorothy was the artist, not him. Click, click. Two of the second fountain.

He'd reached the end of the roll, and the camera whirred as the film rewound. This was the third roll of film he'd finished in as many days. As he reloaded the camera, Walter wondered what he should do with all of the photos. Dorothy would make an album, complete with little notes about the significance of each picture. He'd make an album, too, though without the little notes.

A laughing line of schoolchildren, out on a field trip, crossed the square to his left. Click, click, click. A smiling, red-haired woman biked past the children, whizzing into the third shot. The woman, the bike, and the children meshed in Walter's mind and sparked a memory.

Many summers ago, he, Dorothy, and the kids had vacationed in Chicago. Early one humid morning they rented bikes and pedaled south along the lakefront, Lake Michigan's soft blue rolls to the left of them and row upon row of high-rise buildings to the right. They biked for more than two hours before the kids complained and they stopped for lemonade and salty soft pretzels. Walter closed his eyes and held onto the memory.

"Can you believe this weather?" a woman's voice said at his elbow.

Walter started and turned. One of the elderly sisters—Rose—stood beside him. She looked cold and disgruntled. "I'll never forgive my sister for dragging me to this place," she said.

"Some people like it," Walter said, raising his camera. To the right, an artist was sketching a mother and her young son in charcoal. Click, click of the artist, the mother, and the child.

"You did mention that your wife liked it, didn't you?" Rose said, injecting a note of cordiality in her voice.

"My wife never visited Rome."

"Oh, I'm sorry, I thought you said—"

"She wanted to come," Walter said, staring at the cobblestoned pavement, "but she died before she had the chance."

Rose began muttering condolences that Walter did not hear. He studied the camera, turned it over and over, and fought the sudden urge to smash it to the ground. Why was he taking these pictures? Who were they for? It wasn't even his camera, but Dorothy's. She should be here, not him. For ten years, she talked of coming. But first they had their last child to put through college, then he lost his job for a time, then the house needed work, then her parents needed money, then it was too late.

Rose touched his arm. "I'm going to meet my sister for a cup of coffee. Would you like to join us?"

Walter, still staring at the pavement, nodded. Rose turned and walked toward a rust-colored building with a café on the ground floor. As Walter moved to follow, he saw a young woman of about twenty-five crossing the piazza carrying a large bunch of yellow tulips. A memory. Dorothy coming through the kitchen door, smiling and smelling of earth, bunches of sunflowers in her hands. Walter raised his camera. Click. One of Dorothy.

The Storyteller's Window

by John Saul & Mike Sack

When asked what kind of project they are looking for almost every fiction editor or agent will say, "Give me a good story, well told."

Notice the order of priority: they never ask for "a well-told, good story," nor even "a well-told story." Among most of the editors and agents we have talked to—and there have been quite a few over the past quarter of a century—the *story* is always of primary importance. And a careful study of the marketplace will reveal an interesting fact: while there are many well-known and successful authors who are not exceptionally adept at the skill of writing, they have enormous success based on their astonishing ability to tell a good story. Thus, when the opportunity arose to guide new writers not in the process of writing (which we don't even pretend to know much about), but rather in the process of discovering and developing story ideas, we immediately said "let's go!" (The fact that this process was to take place in Rome certainly didn't make the prospect any less attractive.)

Now, given the above observations of the behavior of editors and agents, it should not be surprising that the single most frequently asked question a novelist hears is this: "Where do you find the ideas for your stories?" The complete answer, of course, has as many variations as there are storylines and writing styles. Yet there is a single common trait that seems to apply to all novelists, the trait from which their storytelling appears to flow. The trait is both simple, and at the same time exceedingly complex. At it's simplest, it is merely this:

Storytellers view the world through a different window from the one used by non-storytellers.

Just as a painter, sculptor or photographer sees things differently from a 'normal' person, so also does the storyteller. Storytellers keep their senses open to everything around them, always keeping a weather eye out for interesting characters, unique locations, peculiar (or seemingly out-of-place) items. Their ears are always listening for sounds of all kinds: odd bits of information or scraps of conversation. Their noses are constantly sniffing for odors that cue something in their minds, and their minds are constantly grinding away, milling the grist their senses are taking in, always with a single specific question in mind: Is there a story here?

That question instantly leads to other questions:

• Am I seeing or hearing or smelling something out of the ordinary?
• Who are the people around me?
• Are they really as they appear?
• What are their relationships?
• Why is that object there?
• How did it get there?
• What would happen if I took this person, and that object, and put them somewhere else?
• What if...?

Consciously or unconsciously, story-tellers are forever peering at the world through this peculiar window, often warped or twisted and always unique to the writer who stands behind it, silently repeating the same words over and over again:

"What if...?"

In our experience, every story idea has germinated from some stimulus. Over the years our novel ideas have come from the evening news, dinner conversations, scientific articles, strange discoveries while traveling, people we've watched or listened to and dozens of other vary-ing stimuli. Much of this data simply passes through, glanced at and discarded, but every now and then some-thing niggles at our minds, and one of us says, "There's a story here." On rare occasions the story is immediately apparent, leaping into our minds fully fledged with a beginning, a middle and an end, a cast of characters and a setting. Far more often, though, while the seed of a story has been planted by some stimulus, that seed has to ger-minate, then incubate for a while until the story begins to take on real form. It is during that period of incuba-tion that a storyteller must delve deeply into the ques-tioning process, and begin discovering the "What if..." from which the entire story will flow.

For the past several years we have been conducting a workshop at the Maui Writers Retreat called The "What If..." Workshop. In the workshop we challenge emerg-ing authors to clarify their story ideas by reducing them to a simple declarative sentence of no more than 25 words, the first two of which are *What If*. While the process is partly intended to help writers communicate their ideas effectively to agents and editors, it goes much further than that: it also helps writers focus on the basic frame-work of their stories and often allows them to determine what form may best suit the story they want to tell. Some "What if..." story lines cry out to be full length novels while others want to be movies or TV series or short sto-ries or even nothing more than a sketch on a comedy show. Some "What ifs..." can even be recognized as rich enough to fill more than one novel and should therefore be considered as the basis for a trilogy or even an ongo-ing series of novels.

"What if..." statements also can clarify the pitfalls of a story as well as define its strengths. Here are some ca-veats we use when guiding the "What if..." workshop:

• The author of a good "What if..." keeps in mind the fact that readers are generally not interested in world peace, corporate intrigue or large organizations. Readers are interested in *individual people* and the extraordinary circumstances surrounding them.

- A good "What if..." identifies the character a reader will care about.
- A good "What if..." states or implies what the conflict will be in the story.
- A good "What if..." answers the two imperative questions any editor will surely ask of any story: Why here? And why now?
- And most important, a good "What if..." communicates what is at stake; what will make the reader keep turning the pages.

Once writers have developed "What if..." statements, they are ready to begin building the stories. It has been our experience that when the "What if..." is weak, the storyline quickly falters and finally peters out entirely. Conversely, when the "What if..." is strong, the story seems to flow easily from the idea. The characters take over and each scene compels the next, with the story unfolding quickly and smoothly.

The Maui Writers Retreat, Italian Style, allowed us to guide thirty-four emerging authors in the process of peering through the storyteller's window to find stimuli that would prompt ideas. The challenge was then to formulate those ideas into solid "What if..." statements for short stories. The final challenge was to complete a first draft of the story within the next twenty-four hours. All in all, not easy challenges for any writer to meet. To make it even more interesting, we asked the writers to work in teams of two until they came up with a strong "What if..." Then they split up, and each of them wrote their own story, giving all of the rest of us two unique peeks through the single window both storytellers had originally used.

What sort of things are writers looking for when they peer through that window? Well, here's an example of just how different we writers are from normal people.

Prior to the beginning of the retreat the leaders were

taken on a tour of the locales we would be using in the days to come. At one point our guide—perhaps the best tour guide in Rome—was discussing the ancient Roman structure in front of us when he noticed that he'd completely lost his audience. All of us—every one of us a writer—had focused not on the building in front of us, but on the object at our feet. It was a woman's coat, black cloth with equally black fake-fur trim. It was used, but not battered, and it was lying in the street. Not on the sidewalk, but on the street itself. One of its sleeves was moving in the gusts of a chill morning wind, almost as if beckoning to us. Those of us with cameras were photographing it, finding it far more interesting than the building upon which Roberto had been discoursing. Questions were already running though our minds: Who had lost this coat? What happened to her that she would abandon a very good coat on a side street in Rome on a blustery morn?

Or had it been lying there for hours?

The stimulus had hit us all, and all our minds had begun grinding away at the possibilities the coat had presented the moment we glimpsed it through our storyteller's window.

Roberto and his building were forgotten.

For the next week thirty-four more writers wandered the piazzas of Rome. Were they looking at the historical structures? Were they awed by the architecture and grandeur? Well, maybe a few were. But most of them were looking at the small things. Meandering into courtyards, peeking into garbage cans, watching people...always watching people. An artist painting a tourist, a gypsy woman hovering near the entrance to an embassy, a solitary nun buying food. They discovered objects as well: leather gloves displayed in a tiny window, a pair of sunglasses lying on a table in front of a café. An unusual flower, a dog leaping in the air next to its owner, a child wandering through a piazza, an old woman sipping cappuccino—all of this was seen through the storyteller's window and all served as germs for stories.

The first step to becoming a storyteller, then, is to begin to look at the world through that special window. The next step is to learn to spot the germs of stories that are glimpsed through the window. From the germ comes the "What if..." and from the "What if..." comes the story.

In Rome thirty-five people discovered how to use the window and make the process work for them. Each of them found an idea, and each of them wrote a story.

And what stories they turned out to be.

The Price of The Pope's Blessing
by Larry Mulkerin

The sign marking the entrance to the village boasted: *Savoca, The Town That Saves its Bodies.*

Mayor Marco Antonio Galducci parked his black Mercedes next to the sign. From there, a mossy brick pathway wound through scrub pines to the Franciscan monastery and the crypt that lay below. The mayor stepped carefully to avoid dirtying his boots or the wide cuffs of his official green uniform. He chose to wear the heavy gold medallion of his office. Marco was prepared to remind his great-great-grandfather that he, Marco Antonio Galducci, was also a man worthy of respect.

Marco hesitated at the door and breathed the scented mountain air before descending into the crypt. Matters of family honor weighed on him and serious family issues always demanded the approval of Marco's great-great grandfather Giuseppe Antonio Galducci. It had been the family tradition to consult him ever since the old bastard was preserved on Christmas Eve, 1888.

At the foot of the stairs, leather-skinned former mayors were suspended in space and preserved in time along the walls of the subterranean hall. Each was supported by wires and preserved by a technique known only to the monks. Over the centuries, the uniforms and the ribbons of recognition became faded and frayed. Reducing the lighting to a dull yellow glow slowed deterioration of the clothing and the mayors, but the lighting conditions forced Marco to blink and wait a few minutes for his eyes to adapt. When his eyes focused, he saw the way that the dried skin of his ancestors contoured tightly to the bones of their skulls and cracked along lines of stress. Their jaws sagged in response to the constant pull of gravity. Each had the kind of gaping, elongated maw that Edvard Munch painted into "The Scream." In other respects, the preservation was remarkable. In all of Sicily it was recognized that God's miracle blessed the Galduccis with great respect.

Marco squared himself in front of his great-great-grandfather and bowed. He raised his head slowly and explained his predicament.

"Great-great-grandpapa, my daughter has reached the age of twenty-six and the doctor says that I will never have a son; there is no possibility. What would you have me do?" Marco Antonio put his ear to the corpse's sagging mouth and said with prayerful reverence, "Can you help me great-great-grandpapa? For the sake of the family name, I beg your assistance." After a minute, Marco began to nod his head and mumble like a penitent in the confessional booth. He snuffled back the wetness in the back of his nose but couldn't stop the escape of a tear. The old patriarch had awakened to help him in his time of distress.

Still touching his ear to the dried lips, Marco sobbed, "What a beautiful idea. *Grazie*, great-great-grandpapa, *molto grazie.*"

He finished by crossing himself and dropping to one knee. Marco kissed his ancestor's desiccated hand. Sadly, he did it with too much fervor. He heard a cracking sound and felt his palms moisten as he opened them and backed away. The corpse's middle finger moved slightly, not sagging toward the floor but extending in his direction until it was straight enough for its intent to be known. Humiliated, Marco dropped his second knee to the floor and pleaded, *"Scuse, scuse."*

Marco crawled backwards on all fours, eyeing the

extended finger. He winced and said, "I have one more question. I must know what boy you would choose for Costanza."

Placing his ear back to the open mouth, he wrinkled his forehead and crossed himself again. "Rossi? That Rossi boy? Great-great-grandpapa, please say it for me again. Maybe, I didn't hear you right." Marco pressed his ear tight against the lips of his slack jawed ancestor but the hollow eyed man had returned to his silent wait for resurrection and judgment.

Marco rose to his feet, stepped back and saluted. He said, "My apologies. You do not have to repeat yourself. It is just that you named Guido 'The Melon' Rossi and that was a surprise. I'll see you next week and I'll bring some nice flowers." Marco grinned at the yawning mouth and offered one more *"Grazie,"* in an appropriate *soto voce* as he backed out the door. He was anxious to tell Guido "The Melon" the wonderful news.

The young man who was called *"Il Melone"* as a boy, had grown out of his rounded face. In fact, Guido Rossi had developed nicely. True, he was too dark and wore his hair much too long to please Marco, and worse, he suffered the Rossi nose, which bent twice, over and back. Sometimes new acquaintances cocked their heads to the side in order to line up with his strange appendage. *Perhaps*, thought Marco, *the boy could see a plastic surgeon after the wedding.* The one thing that Marco Antonio Galducci knew with certainty was that his ancestor Giuseppe Antonio, would not mislead him on a matter of family honor.

The following week, Marco prepared himself in front of a full-length mirror to greet *Signore* Rossi and his son Guido *"Il Melone"* Rossi. The father and son had waited for the mayor for an appropriate half hour in his rose garden. While waiting, Marco had them served fine food and wine in the manner of cultured Sicilians.

Inside, Marco smiled at the fit of his suit and the

splash of gray in his hair, but he asked for his wife's opinion, knowing that it would have been offered anyway.

"You are one grand Sicilian," she beamed. Then she waggled a finger at him, "But, my handsome husband, you must not forget our agreement. Our daughter's union is to be blessed by the pope. You have promised her. Remember that, Marco. It was your promise."

On his way to the garden, Marco stopped to remove a box from the freezer. He carefully removed a black cooler with a gold "G" embossed on both sides and secured with a padlock. He carried it in both hands and put it on the table before grasping his guest's hands and offering his cheeks for kissing.

"I am pleased that you came."

"We have been informed of the purpose of the visit and we are honored."

Marco spoke to the younger Rossi with oozing deference. "Guido. Do you wish to marry my daughter and to show respect in the ways that will be required?"

"But of course. She is very beautiful and," he straightened his back and cleared his throat, "*very* respectable."

Marco narrowed his eyes. "I offer you a chance to join my family. That carries obligations."

The older Rossi stepped toward him. "With great respect, we are also Sicilians and *Sicilians* know the meaning of family. If we did not have strong families, Sicily would not exist."

"Then you will understand my wish that the marriage will involve certain—," Marco paused for effect, shrugged and raised his palms upward. "Let us use the words, certain restrictions."

The Rossis looked for signs of what was coming next and followed Marco's hand to the latch on the cooler.

Marco opened the lid and released a cloud of condensation that cleared to reveal a single, frosted glass tube. "Let me introduce the father of your first child. This has been offered to us by a good and virile Galducci; not too close a relative but one who has fathered eight sons to three women."

Guido tightened his lips and moved his deformed nose to the right and back to the middle. His father put a tight hold on his arm.

Marco responded amiably. "Talk to your father, Guido. He can explain to you that some things are necessary, simply because that is the nature of life here. The main thing to understand is that this is now a family matter."

Guido asked, "No one but we three will know?"

"We three and Costanza. The doctor will know of course because he will perform his service the night before the wedding. I can assure you that neither Costanza or the doctor will ever discuss this matter."

Guido asked, "Can I have some time to consider this?"

"So long as it takes to finish your glass of wine, son-in-law. Families cannot hesitate to help each other, and that will be my promise to you as well." Marco touched his glass to theirs. "*Salud.*"

Marco hugged Guido. "The wedding is scheduled for next month. We could not arrange for the pope's blessing any sooner." He squeezed the young man harder. "We are doing this to please the women but you cannot please my daughter too much before the wedding. You understand?"

To assure that Guido would not do what would normally be expected of a young man, Marco instructed his wife to chaperone all meetings of the couple. Maria Galducci, however, knew one thing that Marco could never comprehend, the desires of their daughter.

The following evening, Guido tapped on the door with flowers in his hand and rubber in his knees. Maria greeted him and directed the lad to sit next to her daughter. Costanza extended her hand. Guido took it with palpable discomfort. Maria said, "I must excuse myself. I will be back in one hour." She pointed to the clock. "One hour exactly."

When she returned, the room was empty. She found Costanza, in her bedroom, lying face down and crying. The girl's chest heaved from her distress.

"Mother of God! Did he hurt you, Costanza?"

"No, but he is not a normal man, mama."

"He is unable to respond?" Maria gave a pumping action of her arm that would have matched her husband's best effort.

"I felt his response but he says to me that he will not touch me until our wedding night."

Maria patted her daughter and pulled her head into the security of her breasts.

"Do I have to marry a man who can so easily refuse me?"

"Give me some time to find out, Costanza."

The cook approached her with a flushed face and asked, "How do you want me to prepare the contents of the cooler and what meal is that to accompany?"

By midnight, Marco was breathing the sighing breaths that accompany dreams and Maria slipped from beneath the sheets and went to the kitchen.

Maria removed the box from the freezer, placed it on the counter. The shackle appeared ready to withstand her best efforts. She cursed and shook her Sicilian fist at the box before hacking a hole in the side with a cleaver. She lifted the tube and read the label, "Human Sperm-Keep Frozen," cursed again and set a pan of water on the stove to cook the offensive ejaculate.

Marco came down the stairs calling, "Maria, what is that racket, woman?" Maria's desire to destroy the tube dissolved into guilt and fear. The only thing that she could do was ask, "Why? Why this, Marco?" but Maria understood. She had not borne a son to a man for whom that was the most important thing in his world. Her best efforts had failed, and despite what the doctor said, it was best thought of as her failure. By morning, the sperm was still safely frozen and Maria had bedded her husband back to sleep.

Maria's backup plan was as simple as human desire itself. Convincing Guido that Sicilians wanted their daughters to marry real men but not to hear the details was the first step. Next she explained to the doctor that it was safer for him to pretend to do the procedure than to actually perform the act. "Besides," she lied, "My daughter is already pregnant. Telling Marco would make him very angry but, on the other hand—," she pointed an accusing finger—"if you hurt the baby that is already in his daughter's belly, he would go insane. There is no way to know what he might do."

A month later, the couple ascended ten marble stairs to the pope's throne, passing between two rows of Swiss guards. A five-year-old girl from the Rossi side of the family held the train for the bride, walking tiptoe in order to raise it as high as she could. Most eyes except those of Marco Antonio Galducci fixed on the determined effort of the charming little girl but even the father of the bride missed one thing. As the couple knelt in front of the pontiff and Guido bent to kiss the papal ring, he slipped his hand to touch Costanza's still flat abdomen. She giggled. The pope saw the move. He smiled and blessed the three of them.

The crypt is now open to the public and for the suggested donation of two euros it is a bargain. A roll of black gauze has been stuffed in the mouth of Giuseppe Antonio Galducci. Attendants will offer varying explanations but all of them agree on one point. Marco had, for some reason, performed the act of stuffing Giuseppe's oral cavity. He had entered the crypt immediately after the birth of his first grandchild. The next morning, Marco was found lying on the floor, clutching the finger of his great-great-grandfather to his chest.

"In Sicily," the attendant will conclude, "We are willing to accept that God works in his own way. Marco, we know, has found peace. He is the one hanging to the left of his great-great-grandfather. See how he smiles."

Visitors should be aware that the crypt is closed on Fridays so that Mayor Guido Rossi and his son, a handsome boy except for his nose, can visit in private.

In the Best Interest of the Child

by Myrna Murdoch

Victoria Mackenzie sat on the Spanish Steps, hugging her knees and thinking what a mistake this trip had been. She needed this time away to get her mind off all that had happened back home in Hawaii, but Rome? What could she have been thinking? She'd honeymooned in Rome. And now, thirteen years later, here she was again, divorced and embroiled in a bitter court battle over custody of Alexandra, her only child. Broken dreams, broken hearts have no place in the Eternal City, she thought.

"Come on, go with me," her sister Jeanne had said. "Sam has Alexandra for Christmas, and the trip won't cost you a cent. It'll be space available, but we'll have fun—it's time you put a little fun back in your life." Jeanne was a United flight attendant with a boyfriend in Rome who had "a brother or a cousin or someone like that" to squire her sister around. "That way you won't feel like three's a crowd." She grinned in that persuasive way she had. "Besides, he's very handsome. And, of course, he's Italian, if you know what I mean."

Victoria did know, and Roberto was all of that. And incredibly nice. She smiled—he would have to be to put up with her and her post-trial angst. It would be different if she didn't have to go back into that courtroom come January third to settle Sam's visitation rights. It might even be different if those honeymoon memories didn't keep popping up.

Everywhere they went, she was reminded of something she and Sam did on their honeymoon. They'd visited the Vatican, of course, and the catacombs. It was the tomb of St. Sebastian, the martyr with all those arrows in his heart that had upset her most. The sight of all that suffering made her own heart bleed. Roberto noticed her tears and quietly handed her a handkerchief. What a drag she was, casting a pall over everything, spoiling everyone's good time.

She'd begged off taking the trip to Assisi today, wanting to give Roberto a day off from his escort duties—and to avoid even more memories. Especially after yesterday, when, quite accidentally, they'd come across the same, obscure gallery where Sam had bought her the fabulous little Monet. She'd never had anything that valuable in her life. He'd showered her with expensive gifts in the early days of their marriage, but everything had been sold to pay for the past seven years of litigation. There was nothing of real value left. She looked down at her empty ring finger, where until recently she'd worn a beautiful ruby wedding ring, the symbol of *"for better or worse, 'till death do us part."*

Sam once vowed she'd be dead and broke by the time it was all over. Well, he was half right. She was nearly broke, but she wasn't dead yet. He'd dragged her into Family Court seventy-nine times, but there was plenty of fight left in her, and no matter what happened, she would never give up on Alexandra. Never. How could she have been so wrong about the man she married? When had he stopped wanting to please her and started taking such delight in torturing her?

Victoria fidgeted as she thought back over her long struggle to have a child her husband didn't want. During the last days of their troubled marriage, she finally became pregnant through *in vitro* fertilization. Alexandra was conceived on September 27, 1990—the single most important day of Victoria's life. And the child was to be hers alone. Sam made her sign an agreement acknowledging that he took no responsibility—basically disowning the baby. Actually, the terms of that agreement had suited Victoria just fine—until Alexandra was about two years old and her father changed his mind and sued for full custody. That was seven years ago, and they'd been in litigation ever since.

He made a convincing show in court—my child this, and my child that—when actually he left Alexandra in the care of servants most of the time. The trouble was that the courts listened to him. Maybe the flow of money passing through sympathetic attorneys' hands eased the deals.

What a disgrace family court was. One judge, who presided over twenty-seven of their hearings, was recently forced off the bench for taking bribes. Anyone else would be in jail, Victoria thought, but that was the court system. There was no doubt in her mind that without his rulings—always in favor of Sam—their case would have been over years ago.

Victoria rose and started down the steps. She had to do something to shake off the overwhelming gloom she'd felt since early this morning. But what? Maybe she'd skip lunch and have a *gelato*. No one made ice cream quite like the Italians, and there was that little shop right next to her hotel.

Whoops! A little girl racing down the steps careened into her, and Victoria teetered, off balance for a moment, before she felt a hand grasp her elbow to steady her.

"I've been watching you," Roberto said. "Can I help?"

Good grief, was she really that obvious? "Do you always go around rescuing ladies in distress?" she asked.

"Only on Tuesdays."

Victoria smiled. It was Thursday.

"Like you, *cara*," he said, "I thought I'd give the others a day by themselves." He took her arm and led her down the stairs. "I have my car near by. Come take a drive with me. It will relax you."

From what Victoria had seen of Roman driving, she

doubted that very much. But it would be a distraction, and she certainly needed that. "Don't you Italians ever work?" she asked.

"It's holiday time, *cara*. Come," he said, and opened the car door for her.

They drove out of the city quite a distance and stopped for lunch at a restaurant built into the side of a craggy bluff. "We'll have time for the gardens at Hadrian's Palace after lunch," he said. "It's very peaceful there. Those old Romans knew how to relax."

Lunch was wonderfully Italian, and Victoria found she was hungry after all. Roberto lived in Milan and was in the textile business. He was good company and regaled her with stories about his family, business, and six-year-old nephew. This was a Roman holiday for him too. His genuine hospitality allowed her to feel he was enjoying the afternoon as much as she was.

They wandered through the gardens at Hadrian's Palace and rested on a stone bench beside the pool. "What is it that troubles you, *cara?*" he asked.

"Have you ever been married, Roberto?"

"Ah, that's it. I haven't been quite honest with you, *cara*. Once upon a time I married an English girl. She was homesick and left me to return to that miserable English climate." He paused thoughtfully for a moment. "The little boy I spoke of is really my son. His name is Guido. Shall I show you his picture?"

"Please do," Victoria said, and she reached in her bag for her own packet of photos. "This is my daughter, Alexandra. She's nine years old." They exchanged admiring parental comments about the pictures of their children, and Victoria began to tell Roberto what it was that dampened her spirits. Finally she said, "So that's my sad story. It went on for seven long years, but I never lost hope. Then this last time, we got a woman judge who was a mother herself. She had enough money and political clout of her own not to be influenced by Sam's distinguished old *kamaiana* family. Shall I tell you about that?"

Roberto nodded and smiled.

"Well, they didn't have all that distinguished a beginning. Rumor has it that Sam's great-grandfather was the *haole* lover of a royal Hawaiian princess. The princess, locked into a childless marriage with a man who was attracted to other men, welcomed the ardent attentions of her *haole* lover and rewarded him with land and power. And, of course, the family wealth and power increased over the years. That's how Sam was able to finance his litigation—to the tune almost a million dollars a year if you can believe that!"

"A sad comment," Roberto said, "on a man who wanted to be absolved of all financial responsibilities for his own child."

"He was niggardly about the settlement also, but I was only too happy to trade away alimony for sole custody. And I'd do it again."

"I see that I'm lucky, *cara*. Averil divorced me, but we're on good terms."

"Thank you for listening to me, Roberto. I feel better now."

"Sit here and rest. I'll get us a *gelato*."

Victoria gave him her most engaging smile. Here, nearly nine thousand miles from home, she had found a friend. "I'd been thinking of that very thing earlier today," she said, "just before you appeared so mysteriously at my elbow."

When Roberto had gone back up the stone stairs, Victoria returned to her thoughts, trying to sort out what she'd do when she returned to Hawaii. Her funds were totally depleted and there was no jewelry left to pawn or sell. But she'd been a successful stockbroker, and although she hadn't worked since her marriage, she knew her old firm would welcome her back. Always one to keep up with the market, Victoria was confident she'd soon be back in stride.

How could that nice judge let Sam have Alexandra for Christmas? Since that terrible Christmas when

Alexandra was five years old, he'd had her every other year. This was supposed to be Victoria's Christmas with Alexandra. Sam had skipped his turn last year to celebrate alone with his new wife. Every time Victoria thought of Alexandra being with him for Christmas this year, the memory of that stolen Christmas burned like a fresh brand on her heart.

When the divorce was finally over, she'd been forced to move herself and Alexandra from the big house they had always lived in to a small two-bedroom apartment. After the move, Alexandra was worried that Santa couldn't find her in their new home, so Victoria helped her fill out a change of address card and mail it to the South Pole. They'd hung Alexandra's Christmas stocking on a chair beside the tree and were just fixing a plate of cookies for Santa when the doorbell rang.

"Mama, come quick!" Alexandra yelled, darting away. "I think it's Santa Claus!"

Victoria wiped sugar from her hands and rushed to join her daughter. Alexandra already had the door open and was looking up eagerly into the face of a big man wearing a uniform.

"You're not Santa Claus," she said.

The uniformed man held a folded legal-looking document.

"This is a secure building," Alexandra said, precocious as always. "How did you get in?"

"Court order, ma'am," the man said, brandishing the document. "I'm the sheriff, and this authorizes me to take the little girl."

Victoria's heart pounded as she told the man there must be a mistake. It was Christmas Eve, and the judge was on vacation. The court was closed until January. It didn't make sense. But not much about family court did. Pulling Alexandra around behind her, she blocked the door.

"No mistake, ma'am," he said, and reaching around Victoria, he grabbed Alexandra by the arm and began half-carrying, half-dragging her down the hall toward the elevator.

"Wait!" she yelled. "Let me see the court order!" But as she quickly scanned the document she saw it wasn't a mistake. A judge she never heard of had signed the order saying Alexandra was to go to her father. It was another of Sam's mean-spirited attacks to upset her, but what about his poor little daughter? Victoria knew for a fact that he wasn't even in town—although he'd been petitioning the court to accept the notion that his maid, one of many, would be his surrogate for the times he was off-island.

She begged to be allowed to get Alexandra's blankie and teddy. "Please," she pleaded, and wedged herself in between the elevator doors to prevent them from closing. "She's never slept without them." At the mention of her beloved blankie, Alexandra, who had apparently been shocked into submission, started to scream. Her howls were deafening and several neighbors came out of their apartments to see what was going on.

"Come on man, give the little girl a break," one neighbor said. "It's Christmas Eve." He tried to grab Alexandra, but the big Hawaiian shoved him roughly away.

Victoria would never forget those elevator doors closing on Alexandra's screams, or how, with those screams echoing in her head, she flew down flight after flight of stairs. All she could think of was getting to Alexandra before she was out of sight. She burst from the stairwell just as the sheriff thrust Alexandra, still screaming, into his car.

She'd made a lunge for the car, but just then the sheriff gunned the engine and a spray of sharp-edged gravel from the driveway flew up in her face. For a moment she was stunned. Then she just stood there, helplessly watching the sheriff's car carry Alexandra away. She couldn't let anything like that happen to Alexandra ever again.

"I hope you like chocolate," Roberto said, holding out a cone covered with sprinkles.

They wandered around the gardens eating their *gelato,* and Roberto asked about the court, explaining that the Italian legal system was different.

"Well," she said. "That last day was just awful. Everyone except the lawyers had to leave the room while they had what's called an "off the record" meeting. I was frightened because it was during those unrecorded meetings that Sam's lawyers had managed to keep me in the kind of custody limbo I'd been in all those years—with nothing really settled."

Banished from the courtroom, she'd paced the hallway and finally went into the ladies' room. She was not encouraged by what she saw in the mirror. At forty-one she still looked young and attractive, but there were haunting dark shadows beneath her eyes.

She hadn't been sleeping well. If she won, she and Alexandra had something to celebrate. If . . .what a big word that was.

It was warm that day, even for Hawaii. She moistened a paper towel in the cool running water and pressed it against the pulse points in her neck. Drying her hands, she again noticed how bare her ring finger looked without the ruby, the last of her jewelry to go. She didn't really care about the ring, and she enjoyed the irony that it was her opponent who'd given her the means to fight him. At first she'd represented herself in court, *pro se,* they called it, but soon learned that was a mistake.

Victoria remembered smiling to herself in the mirror, a little grimly, and telling herself to cheer up. After all, with a woman judge on the bench things just might go her way this time. She picked up her bag and returned to the foyer, thinking about her plan to spirit her daughter away to Australia if she lost custody.

"But you won," Roberto said.

"Yes. I had a wonderful lawyer, one of the best in Honolulu, and I felt guilty about that Australia business. He would never have approved of my plan to flee the state's jurisdiction. He might even have gotten in trouble over that himself. I felt badly about it, but I think I would have done it." She sighed.

"When we went back into the courtroom it was filled with attorneys and clerks, all making very busy with stacks and stacks of papers. They are very good at shuffling papers. I didn't know what to expect and asked my lawyer what was happening. He smiled mysteriously and said, 'The judge is ready to rule.' I was speechless. My heart pounded. After seven years of that torture, finally, in just a few minutes, it would all be over. All I could think to say was, 'This is it?'"

Roberto laughed. "Famous last words," he said. "What did your lawyer say?"

Victoria laughed with him. "He said, 'This is it!' I know it sounds dumb, but I was so scared. And then suddenly there was a commotion in the back of the room. The door opened and Alexandra came in. I wondered what was going on. The children involved rarely appear. Alexandra had never been sent for in the past. It was very scary.

"I felt a tremor go through me, and that metallic taste of fear was in my mouth. My attorney reached over and took my hand, but I hardly noticed. I think I was in a state of shock. All I could think about was my child. The judge began by saying hello to Alexandra and asking her to sit in the chair by the court reporter. My mind seemed to freeze, and the judge droned on and on. I could hear her words, but I couldn't grasp their meaning. Alexandra's face was turned away from me toward the judge.

"Then the judge said '*In the best interest of the child*,' and her gavel made a loud, banging sound on the *koa* wood bench. That startled me, and I sort of came to, wondering what she thought was in the child's best interest. Then I heard the crash of Alexandra's chair overturning, and she flew across the room and launched herself into my arms, saying 'We won, Mama, we won! The judge says I can stay with you!' I finally realized what had happened. Tears of relief ran down my cheeks, and I gathered Alexandra up and held her like I'd never let her go. There was pandemonium in the courtroom as my family all rushed in, and we all laughed and hugged our lawyer. One of Sam's many lawyers approached and shook hands with ours. Legal protocol they call it. What an amazing bunch those lawyers are."

Victoria paused, remembering her final moments in the courtroom. "I looked around for Sam to see how he was taking defeat, but he'd already left the room. And it was then I realized I no longer hated him. Suddenly I felt free of all the rancor of the past, and I only pitied him. In spite of all the wealth and power he'd used against me, I had won Alexandra, and he didn't even know what it really was that he'd lost."

"I can't imagine that, *cara*. Family here in Italy is everything."

Victoria laughed. "That's not the way we hear it," she said.

"Ah, but it's so. We Italian men have earned our reputation, but we value our children above everything else."

Victoria looked deeply into Roberto's eyes and believed what he said. She too valued her child above everything else. "Now all that's left is his visitation hearing, which will take place when I go home."

"Will you come back to Italy some day, *cara*? May I come to Hawaii to visit you?" Roberto handed Victoria some *lire* to wish upon, then toss into the Trevi fountain.

Victoria wasn't sure that was a good idea. They were both parents, but other than that, she and Roberto were worlds apart. Nevertheless, he'd been a good friend to her and in other circumstances, who could say. "You never can tell, Roberto," she said, as she tossed a coin. "In Hawaiian, *aloha* means hello as well as goodbye."

A Few Coins

by Mark Sylvester

The baby appeared to be sleeping with his legs and arms hanging limply over the edges of a box. A few coins were scattered on the cardboard beside him. I tried not to stare, but the gypsy mother sat with her back against the wall. Her legs lay across the walkway and the box with the child in it lay across her lap. Cars flew past on the narrow cobblestone street as I approached, leaving only enough room for a prayer between the spinning wheels and the woman's soil-stained feet.

I stopped and faced a shop window, turning just enough to see the two figures at the concealing edge of my wraparound sunglasses. A feeling of uneasiness twisted my stomach into knots. Something was not right. In my medical training, in a border city of the United States, I had seen children drugged and used as instruments for sympathy before, but more was at stake in this instance. Was it the pale olive of the child's skin, the nearly undetectable rise and fall of its chest, or the lack of any other movement? He seemed balanced on the edge of a precipice, needing only a careless breeze or an unforgiving nudge to send him over the edge and into the abyss where children never grow older.

The mother's face, lined with fine wrinkles, told of a life of hardship and pain. At first, I could not see her eyes, only the darkened hollows that encased them. I turned away and stared into my reflection in the window as if to ask what I should do. What *could* I do? Over the years, my instincts had become my best allies and they were crying out to me. But only a blood test would tell if the child had been drugged to the edge of death to make it appear ill and an easier target for compassion. And I was in a country where I could not speak the native language, was unfamiliar with the begging culture and could easily end up imprisoned, convicted of a murder I had tried to prevent.

I backed away from the window and turned to walk in the opposite direction. The image of the nearly lifeless child became more distinct in my mind the further I moved down the street. I could almost feel his skin growing cold. I crossed over the cobblestones but could go no further. My legs were weak and gave way as I slammed into the lower facade of a building, coming to rest on an outcropping of marble. I didn't want to look up. I wished to be thousands of miles away, back in the comfort of my home where my own child was healthy and not on the edge of darkness.

The shadows moved across my feet as I stared at the worn stones below them. I felt helpless and hollow. Did the Hippocratic Oath apply to this situation? I was torn between the need to save the child's life and the fear of losing my own. I heard a cry from the child's direction and looked up. Its hands were flailing. The women seemed to be scolding the child in Italian and slapping it. Each blow only intensified the cries. I clinched my hands into fists and watched the blood drain from my fingers. A chill raced up my spine. The cries continued.

A desperate, higher pitched scream blasted through the narrow street, followed by gasps and coughing. The woman offered her breast but the baby pushed it away. She shoved a bottle between his lips but he spit it back. Grabbing the baby's head, she crammed the bottle deeper into his mouth. He gagged and coughed then began taking long draws from the bottle as if trying to breathe through it. Every muscle in my body tensed in anger but would not allow me to rise to my feet. A paralyzing terror swept over me, leaving me to watch my tears mixing with the dirt below. An eerie silence followed, interrupted only by the passing scooters and cars.

As my muscles relaxed, I looked up. The woman was bent over the child, her back hunched forward and her head teetering on her neck. I thought she might be asleep until I saw her shoulders jerking. She leaned back against the wall and wiped her eyes with her scarf.

I jumped to my feet and ran toward her. She appeared not to notice me until I was just a few feet from the shop window. Her eyes were filled with terror and pain. She clutched the box and bolted as I reached out and grabbed the baby's foot. It was cold and blue. Suddenly, I was tackled from behind and the lifeless mass jerked from my hand. The woman's dress disappeared around the corner as my outstretched arms and chin crashed into the cobblestones.

As I came to, an elderly lady knelt beside me and held a cool cloth to my forehead.

"What happened?" I felt the words form on my lips.

"You fall and no move," she said. I felt the warmth of her kind eyes.

"Who hit me?"

She shrugged her shoulders. People, gathered nearby, began to walk away.

"Did you see the woman with the child?" I asked, hoping it had been a dream but knowing better.

She shook her head. "Best you go now. *Polizia* come soon. Not good for you."

I stood, slowly walked to the corner and called a cab. As I slipped into the back seat, I realized the child was dead, its life snuffed out and the question of my guilt would haunt me the rest of my life.

For the remainder of the day and all through the night, I could not warm the hand that touched the lifeless, icy foot. I lay on my bed and stared at the ceiling until it eventually faded into darkness. The mother's eyes haunted me with their excruciating pain. Hours moved slowly. Why does any society exist where a life has to be placed in the face of death for others to live?

In the morning, I crawled off the bed and put on my shoes. I had not removed my clothes from the day before. I took a cab back to the *Campo di Fiori* and sat outside a coffee shop. Later, as the beggars began to appear, I walked to the corner where I had sat paralyzed and leaned past the building to see the shop window. I inched further. Just beyond the reflection of the glass stood the old lady who had comforted me, with her arm around another. I looked closer. The other woman was the gypsy who had been with the child. Her eyes had a dull glaze over them as if molting, shedding an old skin. Her face looked cold and hard. There were no little arms and legs, only an empty, battered box clasped in weathered hands.

I wondered if the coins were still in the box and if they had been worth it.

The Empty Chair

by Diana Rowe Martinez

Thirty-five thousand feet above my problems, I decided that losing a husband is like losing your balance. Since we had honeymooned in Italy, flying to Rome seemed a perfectly illogical place to get over my Sam's untimely death. Yet here I was, as usual, imbalanced and impractical but determined. So far my accomplishments consisted of leaving my hotel and crossing the bustling *Campo di Fiori*. I zigzagged through the piazza filled with locals bartering among vendors for their share of the rainbow-colored produce. At a quaint sidewalk café, I found a place to pretend to relax and met the widow who talked to her dead husband.

I watched the elderly woman walk through the café as if performing a ritual. She leaned on a cane decorated with a gold lion's head, but it didn't slow her down. She had purpose behind her slow gait, and her blunt cut, silvery hair danced across her shoulders. She wore a flattering Gucci suit, matching purse, and jewelry that surely weighed more than her slight frame. I judged her to be in her late seventies, perhaps older by the way she walked and her heavily creased laugh lines.

The woman's kind blue eyes met mine. She nodded and gave me a small understanding smile. I looked away quickly. I wore no make up, and I knew my eyes were reddened from tears that still came too easily.

The moment the staff noticed the elderly woman,

there was a flutter of activity. A tall, black-haired maître d' greeted her. *"Buon giorno, Signora* Farago. *Signore* Farago is waiting for you at your usual table."

"Grazie, Marco," she said and handed him a few coins. Combining her distinctive English accent with her fair skin and a profile that did not carry the typically Roman nose, I assumed she was British.

The woman was escorted to an unoccupied corner table close to my own where a waiter held her chair out. She sat down and hooked the cane on the table corner. The young man grinned at her, turned to the empty chair, bowed and said a few words in Italian that I couldn't quite understand before he rushed inside. Within seconds, another young waiter placed a steaming cappuccino and pastry in front of her and in front of the empty chair. He repeated the process of speaking to the woman and then to the empty chair before he, too, left.

Signora Farago smiled in the direction of that chair, placed a spoonful of sugar in her cup and then in the one across from her. When she began speaking animatedly, my heart ached for this lonely woman and I wondered what had caused her to cross that imperceptible line.

Oh I understood "lines" all too well, for I was guilty of talking to an empty house full of shadows and memories—although I could never admit that to my daughter. Bless her heart, my daughter already thought I was losing it—no sense giving her more reason to commit me. The elderly woman was too well dressed to be crazy, but how well I appreciated that insanity knew no financial boundaries.

"Americano caffe, signora." The waiter placed the steaming cup in front of me.

"Scusi, por favore." I stopped the waiter and then switched back to English and pointed to the woman, not really expecting him to answer. "Who is she talking to?"

After glancing over his shoulder, the waiter responded, "Her husband." He shrugged his shoulders in that expressive Italian way as if surprised that I didn't know, and he scurried on to the next customer without giving me the opportunity to question him further.

Was I missing something here? Was I the only one who thought talking to someone that wasn't there reeked of not-quite-right? The thought hit home and frightened me. I still found myself talking to Sam as if he were right beside me. Thirty-odd years of habit, I had supposed, but now I became concerned. Was my destiny looking me in the face in the form of this elderly English/Italian widow?

When *Signora* Farago reached across the table and patted the tablecloth as if it were someone's hand, I recalled how I used to do that with Sam. I'd stroke his palm during breakfast, usually absently, while reading the newspaper. Sheer panic streaked through my blood at the unbidden memory.

Dear God, could I be staring in the mirror?

The woman's tinkling laughter echoed infectiously across the piazza, and her facial features relaxed. As she continued speaking to the empty chair, she appeared at least twenty years younger than when she had arrived.

I remembered how Sam had made me laugh out loud, a belly laugh, something I hadn't done since he died three months ago. The thought of my husband relaxed me ever so slightly, and I sat back in my chair, for once feeling the warmth of the sun beating down on my bare face.

The cafe began to bustle with a mid-day rush, and I moved my chair to continue watching the woman. A potpourri of visitors stopped by her table, some old, some very young. All greeted her and the empty chair. I didn't really know what to make of that apparent acceptance of delusion, but I was in a foreign country. Who knew what was acceptable here?

The woman picked up her cup and sipped, her little finger extended in appropriate British etiquette. I smiled to myself. A southern lady, I had been taught to do the correct bend of the pinkie, too, and how Sam used to tease me about that. He'd threatened to tape my finger down and then see if I could continue to drink my tea.

I had pushed his memories to the back of my head for so long that the nostalgia felt good, and deliciously naughty. Something my heart fought for and my mind fought against.

When another local blocked my view, I slid my chair more to the right. This time, the woman reached across the table and appeared to caress the air as if brushing against her husband's cheek.

I closed my eyes, remembering Sam's strong jaw line, his salt-and-pepper hair, his brown eyes, the feel of his roughened beard against the back of my hand. I could see him as clearly as if he were beside me. I could feel him in my heart as if he had never left.

My eyelids flickered. If I repeated these actions at home—talking and touching my invisible husband, my daughter would have me in therapy. Was I destined to be like this crazy old woman? And why did society urge us to forget something our hearts take so long to memorize?

Signora Farago spoke again to the empty chair and rose unsteadily to her feet. She knocked her cane onto the floor, teetered back into her seat, and attempted to retrieve it from underneath the table.

The café was so busy that the waiters did not notice her struggles. Without another thought, I stood. I recovered the cane and handed it to her.

She did not seem surprised to see me. "I wondered if you'd gather the courage to talk to me. May I introduce you to my husband?" She waved her hand toward the empty chair. "Franco, I told you this young lady needed me."

I was incredulous. She truly believed her husband sat across from her. For some reason it bothered me, even angered me, that she had her husband with her even if only in her own imagination, and I had nothing but empty houses and lonely vacations. "Excuse my bluntness, *signora*," I said, not feeling a bit of remorse at dashing the woman's fantasy to pieces, "but please tell me you know that there is no one in that chair."

She threw her head back and laughed that rich laughter. Her heavily ringed fingers fluttered near her throat. "I bet you think I'm quite mad, don't you?"

I could only nod. Of course I did. What concerned me was that I was undertaking the same journey.

"Please sit down and join me, my dear." I headed to the empty chair, but she stopped me with a wave of her hand. "Pull up another chair, why don't you?"

I obeyed. After all, I had nowhere else to be and no one else to talk to, not anymore.

"You've lost your husband recently, haven't you?"

"How could you know that?" Aside from the forever-red eyes and dejected slope to my shoulders, I didn't think it was blatantly obvious.

"You have that haunted look about you, like you're trying to forget someone impossible to forget." She patted my arm, and her hands were soft, cool and comforting. I resisted clinging to them. "My dear Franco has been gone for ten years next month, and I've never been able to forget him. He was a good man, although a bit trying at times. After nearly a year of mourning him and trying to badger myself into getting on with my life, I realized I was going about it all wrong."

"Wrong? Excuse my bluntness, *signora*, but pretending he sits in the chair surely can't help." Call me old-fashioned, but I still slotted delusional in the crazy category.

"Ah, but my dear, it does. When you've spent as much time with a man as I had with Franco, and he is the only life you've ever known, remembering is bittersweet but as necessary as breathing."

"But why do you talk to him as if he sits across from you? And the others, why do they go along with it?"

"The others think I'm a crazy, old lady and are simply amusing me. Oh, and I'm quite well off—that certainly lends motivation." She chuckled. "But I'm not crazy, truly. I only talk to Franco here, my dear. Oh, there are times when I catch myself talking to him at home—it's hard to break a habit, you know, but this one place I give myself permission to remember him and cherish his memory. And not feel guilty about it."

"Here? Why here?"

"Because this café is where we first met. Isn't that right, Franco?" Her face glowed with the beauty of decades of laughter and love. "He swept me off my feet that day and every day for the entire fifty-one years we were together. He also irritated the hell out of me. And here, once a week, he continues to do so, and I let him."

My southern gentry upbringing still protested. "But why not at home, somewhere where others don't observe your..."

"My madness?" She smiled and then sighed. "Because this place, in that empty chair, in this café, is the only place he comes alive for me." Her hand slid across the table and she clutched the imaginary one of her husband. "You need to find your special place to remember your husband, my dear, for it's in those precious memories that we can go on living."

I felt chills run down my back. I knew exactly the place where I could find Sam again. "*Grazie, Signora, piacere.* You have no idea what a pleasure it is to meet you." I took her ringed fingers in mine and squeezed.

"Oh my dear, believe me, I know exactly how you feel. Now go on. Franco and I have some catching up to do."

Within five minutes, I had walked to the taxi stand and directed the driver to the Fountain of Trevi. The late morning sun tinted the statues a welcoming golden hue. Sam and I had been so young, eager for life, eager to spend our lives together, and this was the first, and the last, place we had visited on our honeymoon so many years ago. And this was the only place I'd promised myself I'd avoid while in Rome.

I descended the steps, stood near the middle of the fountain and closed my eyes, and opened myself to his memory. The mid-week crowd flowed around me, and the water gently cascaded to its own rhythm, lulling me into those remembrances of Sam and how we had wrapped our arms around each other, our backs to the fountain, and each tossed a coin. Legend proclaimed that the fountain possessed the power to bring visitors back to Rome, and we had wanted to return together.

"Oh Sam, here you are," I said, to the air, and I felt the gentle, reassuring hush of his presence. The breeze teased my hair, blowing it onto my check, and I allowed myself to think and remember without an ounce of guilt, at this moment and this special place, my husband.

Fire in the Eternal City
by Janette Ressue

"Burn it!" he exclaimed, staring her squarely in the eyes. If optically induced internal combustion applied to novice writers as well as fantasy novel characters, she might have instantly imploded into a pile of ashes upon the five star hotel's sparkling Italian marble floor. Instead, a wry smile crossed her face as she averted her green-eyed gaze, gliding a stricken, yet steadfast, left index finger northwesterly across the warm smoothness of the mouse pad, closing the shared file following a swift tap to the save icon. Under left cortex control in its logical prowess, her gentle right hand quietly lowered the computer screen to kiss the keyboard, fully concealing the fate of her juvenile rhyming-couplet poem, the fruit of her second Roman writing assignment. Compared to the sweet succulent words already shared by her writing retreat cohorts, who continued to inspire and delight her senses with their savory gourmet concoctions amazingly blended to completeness within less than twenty-four hours, hers in sour contrast commanded only blank stares, a few piteous looks and deafening silence from the circularly seated well-seasoned group. Realistically speaking, what could possibly follow the master author's infliction of the potentially fatal two word utterance, for in declaring her work unfit for consumption and a creation any discerning publisher would most violently spit out rather than devour or invest in, he had more profoundly proven in complete brevity, the tenant that less *is* truly more. Unless of course the "less" is a short story constrained within the decidedly tedious form of rhyming line poetry, cheating readers of the amalgamation of multi-sensory imagery, conflict and unique Roman inspiration that fueled its conception. Dagger expertly inserted, its figurative point absorbed like aloe into scaly dry skin, the depths of her logical mind were indeed grateful, while the rest of her secretly wished to be engulfed by the smooth flowing darkness of a velvet invisibility cloak. To her dismay, such protective garments were also accessories reserved exclusively for fantasy novel characters, juveniles most likely, leaving novice writers to twist in the wind or mature quickly in the face of adversity. Her mental scoreboard now broadcasting 0-2 standings for the week as the initial caress of a growing breeze brushed her cheek, she winced sharply realizing that had she donned the fanciful Italian coat purchased on excursion the previous day, she would have at least had the comfort of a furry black synthetic surrogate pet to sink her chipping manicured nails into, avoiding the recent subcutaneous puncture of at least a capillary or two in her right arm during this salient moment of terror and self-induced failure, garnished to perfection with a sprig of public humiliation.

An unexpected spark from her flint-laden composition bringing the morning session to a heated close, protective arms embraced the culprit computer and its provocative contents tightly against her smoldering chest as she entered the vacant mirror-lined elevator that instantly filled to capacity with her swirling thoughts and emotions. As it rose, routing escape to her princess lair for a bit of respite before the afternoon tour of "Ancient Rome", her spirits quickly followed as she thought her poem in combination with failed assignment number one, the "Grand Opera" outline, could at least provide some kindling to fuel the roasting of chestnuts in a lively Roman piazza that evening. What an unusual flavor that batch might have laced within their warm mealy softness, sliding with unique melodic ease down the esophageal passages of unsuspecting tourists and locals alike. Oral fixation obviously mounting, as the pangs in her turned stomach crescendoed to an audible growl, she gave herself a wink and a smile as she knew this was precisely the occasion for breaking out the nine dollar jar of cashews residing patiently within her fittingly five-star computerized mini bar. Obviously a "Type-A" appliance, this modern day marvel of cutting edge sensory technology beamed the equally astounding charges directly to one's bill, allowing a mere thirty seconds of indecision once the desired item was lifted from its designated roost of temptation. She entertained a fleeting wisp of consolation realizing that if by the grace of God and the Pope's Holy-Week blessing she osmotically obtained enough knowledge and inspiration to position an original composition within the retreat publication, it would all be tax deductible in the end.

Upon entering the tranquil safety of her elegantly sundrenched room, decorated in pleasing warm yellows and deep royal blues, she drew a bath, several performance-style operatic breaths and descended into the steaming liquid bubbling with a sweet floral aroma that instantly calmed her steel nerves and allowed quiet reflection on the events of her inaugural writing experience halfway to completion. What a perfect setting Rome provided, as today's session fittingly took the form of an ancient gladiatorial spectacle. Amidst a palpable air of excitement and nervous tension, each fatigued yet determined gladiator entered the arena's center floor wielding a vast array of exotic weaponry to be challenged by the master and judged by the crowd with one universal question to be answered. Would the skill and artistry of their prose win their freedom, prized authorship, or would they continue to be slaves to unpublished manuscripts destined to become literary fatalities? In the case of the novice, another more crucial question remained uniquely hers, for she had entered the arena in naive greenness with essentially no weaponry beyond a strong will, an insatiable thirst for challenge and growth and a guiding philosophy that consulting the experts was the most valuable path toward efficient exploration of any new terrain for the serious minded, not to mention a probable dash of ignorance regarding this venue. Would the skillful jabs of the masters combined with the treachery of the unsuspected wild animals that leapt from trap doors below, destroy or deepen her desire to persevere in crafting her own unique strategic weaponry, the intensity of this experience producing perhaps a new line of ingenious battle tactics that might eventually turn the resounding boos of the spectators into a cheering ovation and a few future royalties? More specifically, in response to the detonation of the morning's explosive two-word utterance, would the creation of kindling this week spark the true creative flame of a budding writer? The answers, she believed, were slowly emerging as this unprecedented experience progressed, for among the dark looming clouds of failure, she spied a thin glistening strain of silver.

A fascinating tour of Ancient Rome and full day excursion to Pompeii now under her belt, she awakened with a harrowing jolt, feet thrust violently from beneath the soft covers to dangle momentarily at the side of a seemingly nightmare-ridden king sized bed. A heaving sigh of relief ensued as familiar surroundings came into view and she pondered momentarily the fascinating nature of the subconscious mind in its ability to bizarrely blend conscious experiences and ideas, especially in the early morning dream state. Auditioning for the role of horror story generator this week, her subconscious had produced an early morning mosaic thriller featuring the bad poetry squad, headed by five torch-bearing master authors, who were escorting their novice fair-haired victim to a specially crafted five-foot, five-inch horizontal opening deep within the dark eerie dampness of the Roman catacombs. Gorged to the eyeballs with pasta, plates of still-on-the-bone meat, and fried-alive fish she was forced to ingest at her "Last Supper," while her classically-trained ears were tortured by the high volume strains of amateur opera grating on the last of her accomplished musical nerves, she stood at the mercy of her foes now poised to grant her one final wish, the company of her beloved black coat, when the unexpected eruption of Mt. Vesuvius distracted them long enough for her to make a run for it, a few stray dogs and fashionably dressed sleek Italian suitors at her heels. In its over stimulated state, her particular subconscious could indeed be a creative, if not twisted, entity whose currently ludicrous fervor might be harnessed for a few practice short stories upon returning to the beauty of the island paradise she called home. A wondrous place where even the onions were sweet, Maui was a familiar delight on the horizon, although she could not stifle the growing ache of melancholy sprouting from the realization that the final writing excursion was upon her, as she rose to ready herself for the last Roman hurrah.

Sometimes the silver lining within her storm clouds remained faint and elusive, while at other times it nearly blinded her. Had intuition forewarned her of the beacon forthcoming, she would have selected a sleek black pair of Italian designer sunglasses to compliment her fashion ensemble of the day. The vibrant unmistakable glow seemed to emanate from out of nowhere as the last author pair provided their prologues to this final writing adventure, an excursion designed to fill each writer's cabinet with the multi-sensory delights of *Piazza Navona*. As Michelangelo, in his brilliant rebellious genius, created larger-than-life images in the Sistine Chapel's exclusive forward chamber, allowing the less privileged societal subjects privy only to the aft section to be equally inspired by his artistry, so did the red-haired author's words reach the novice among the seasoned unveiling the belief that all great literature was born of bad poetry.

Woven in amongst the shiny threads of her current quirky photography craze, astute people watching and conversation eavesdropping skills, and the incessant character and plot lines that punctuated her slumber, a brilliant now swatch-sized lining of gleaming platinum graced the gray mass that hovered above her, illuminating the discernable beak of a Phoenix emerging from the pile of ashes created in the same seated circle several days earlier. How fitting that her favorite feathered friend who never deserted her in a time of adversity, should arrive during Holy Week in Rome she thought, viewing the private scene of resurrection with a secret smile.

As she entered *Piazza Navona* later that morning, a freshness of renewal in the air mixed with the scent of baking pizza dough and warm brewing cappuccinos, she peacefully drank in the beauty of the scene with its adorning frescos, expertly sculpted fountain and abounding lively human interactions. After reluctantly seating herself for a portrait, part of another emerging life plot, a plethora of images and characters swirled by occupying the racing mind encased within her now visually scrutinized external vessel. Her heart was in an instant completely stolen by the curious wide blue eyes of a handsome dark wispy haired Italian toddler, who gazed with wonder upon everything in his view, following gleefully the dancing bubbles secreted by the battle guns of the local street vendors. As his unsteady legs met uneven cobblestones, creating an intersection of momentary collapse and pain, she knew he was indeed a kindred spirit as he promptly righted himself setting out for the next exploration unscathed by the brief setback. What she knew for certain, seemingly intuited by the street artist's sketch of her evolved expression, was that she would never again be the same. And, for the price of a small used car when all was said and done, she had somehow managed to finally forge the exciting new path of adventure her ailing cerebral cortex had so desperately desired. *Perfecto!*

It was not until final arrival at Maui's tropical open-air baggage claim that she fully appreciated the red-haired author's three word novel opener, "Death changes everything." as her precious computer contents guarded with ferocious fervor during the three plane journey home were knocked to the concrete by an overzealous over liquored tourist, the hard drive cushioning the blow. Indeed, the humble chronicle of her first writing adventure might never have been born had her laptop not been so recklessly and fatally bludgeoned. To the bumbling tourist, not to mention the master authors, retreat organizers, cohort writers, and fabulous Roman tour guides, she was undyingly grateful. As for the fate of her poem, a saved printed copy magically still in hand, she thought if emitted from the lips of a tragic female character set to one of the constantly swirling harmonious melodies that accompanied her daily existence, it might just provide a unique musical compact disc supplement to a forthcoming novel strategically marketed in concert together within a brilliant silver package. For Rome, after all, remains the Eternal City.

The Contributors

Elva Adams teaches High School English in New York's Mid Hudson Valley. She has been writing short stories and other fiction since 1994, and has just completed the first draft of a novel. The inspiration for this short story came from observing the market square at *Campo di Fiori* in Rome and noticing the closed shutters in the surrounding buildings. Additionally, she followed the "what if" process taught by authors John Saul and Michael Sack at the Maui Writers' Conference in Maui, Hawaii. *What if a lonely spinster, seduced by the quaint shuttered façade of a hotel, checks in only to find out it is infested by vampires?*

Susan Agee has lived in or around Memphis, Tennessee since 1971. She shares her home with the beautiful but cranky Mr. Kitty, to whom she owes her habit of waking at 3 a.m. to write. Her hobbies include reading and collecting frequent flyer miles.

Dorothy Allison is the author of *Bastard Out of Carolina*, a finalist for the 1992 National Book Award, and *Cavedweller* (Dutton, 1998) a national bestseller and a New York Times Notable Book of the Year, as well as the memoir *Two or Three Things I Know for Sure* (Dutton, 1995). *Trash*, a collection of her short fiction, will be published in a Plume edition fall, 2002.

Kathleen Antrim is a former columnist for the ANG Newspaper Group in the San Francisco Bay Area. She now focuses on novel writing. She lives in Pleasanton, California with her husband and two daughters, and is currently at work on her third novel. Her first novel, *Capital Offense* is scheduled for release in September, 2002. The kernel of a story that became "Torn" was conceived during an audience with the Pope at the Vatican, while she watched tentative brides and grooms prepare for a marital blessing.

Olivia Barbee has more than seven years of experience as a professional nonfiction writer. She is currently at work on her second novel. This piece was inspired in part by the pressure that friends put upon her, a non-photographer, to bring back lots of pictures of her Rome trip.

Mary Ann Brock has twice won first place awards in the SWA's novel and romance novel competitions. She has published several articles and has had stories and poems published in literary anthologies. She is a vice president of Eddie Rents, Inc., and lives in Rome, Georgia— the sister city of Rome, Italy—with her husband Ed.

Terry Brooks was born in Sterling, Illinois, in 1944. He received his undergraduate degree from Hamilton College, where he majored in English Literature, and his graduate degree from the School of Law at Washington & Lee University. A writer since the age of ten, he published his first novel, *The Sword of Shannara*, in 1977. It became the first work of fiction ever to appear on the New York Times Trade Paperback Bestseller List, where it remained for over five months. He has written nineteen novels since, has sold over fifteen million copies and is published worldwide. He teaches annually at the Maui Writers Conference & Retreat and lectures extensively on the craft of writing. He lives with his wife Judine in the Pacific Northwest and Hawaii.

Joni Barron Brotherton has fashioned a new career for herself writing fiction after twenty-five years of writing business and technical articles for corporate America. She is a seventeen-year resident of Maui where she lives with her two cats and enjoys frequent visits with her children and grandchildren.

Carolyn Buchanan lives in Auburn, Alabama with her husband Jerry and her two sons. Her award winning short stories have been published in the *Georgia Writer's Inc.* newsletter, *Allilitcom* literary magazine, and *Ordinary and Sacred As Blood: Alabama Women Speak.* Carolyn has attended the Iowa Summer Workshop, and is a three-time attendee of the Maui Writer's Retreat and Conference. She is currently working toward her MFA in Creative Writing at Antioch University in Los Angeles.

Judith K. Clements lives on the beautiful high desert in Bend, Oregon. She lives with her husband and near her son and daughter-in-law, and practices as a psychologist. She is working on her second novel.

Barbara de Normandie lives on an island in the Pacific Northwest with her husband of twenty-three years and three children. After almost a decade in the computer industry, she turned her attention to raising her children, volunteering extensively in educational and writing organizations, traveling, and establishing a place for herself in the world of authors.

Phillip Dibble has been writing for lots of years, mostly articles for medical journals. Now it's time for fiction. He lives to travel and gather data for stories. He lives with his wife in Mission Hills, Kansas.

Elizabeth Engstrom has written seven books, including *Lizzie Borden, Lizard Wine,* and most recently, *Suspicions,* and has edited four anthologies. She teaches the fine art of fiction in the Pacific Northwest where she lives with her husband and dog. She is the director of the Maui Writers Retreats and the Maui Writers Conference Department of Continuing Education.

Robin Field Gainey, a native of Washington State, returned to Seattle in 1992 after helping to establish a family vineyard in Santa Barbara County, California. She spent time abroad living in Rome with her two daughters before remarrying and settling back in Seattle for good, where she continues to live with her children, her husband and her dogs.

Christopher Sirmons Haviland lives in White Plains, New York with his wife whom he met on the internet. He co-produced an independent feature film in 1997 called The First of May, starring Julie Harris, Mickey Rooney and the late Joe DiMaggio. He has written five screenplays and has completed the first of a series of epic science fiction novels and is novelizing one of his fairy tale screenplays. Besides writing, he enjoys genealogy, paleontology and the internet, and was a startup staff member of About.com and Mail.com. This is his first published short story, inspired by the fountains of Rome and the beggars that live near them.

Octavia Hudson is a screenwriter, former television journalist, documentary producer, talk show host and aspiring novelist. She found the Rome retreat inspiring. This piece was a result of the dreaded Sack and Saul "What If" exercise that turned out to be more helpful than painful.

Ann Klein divides her time between homes in Portland and Cannon Beach, Oregon, with her two teenage children, two Siberian huskies, and a Himalayan. Any time remaining is devoted to her two passions: writing fiction and studying *The Collected Works of C.G. Jung*. "The Antique Typewriter" was inspired by a "what if" exercise which started on the Spanish Steps in Rome but ended in front of an antique shop window.

Sandra Loera and her husband reside in San Diego where they miss their two daughters who insist on being New Yorkers. Stepping where another has walked before has always given her a sense of connection between the past and the present.

Adrea Mach, a journalist and communications professional with the United Nations and the World Health Organization, publishes regularly on international development issues. She began writing creative non-fiction and poetry, coupled with photography, in 1998. "The Invisible Necklace" is her fiction debut. Born in the United States, Adrea has spent most of her adult life in Europe, and currently lives in Geneva. *What if an errant seeker was able, 'in the company of angels,' to let go of self-destruction and embrace peace, enlightenment—and people?*

Diana Rowe Martinez is a freelance writer by day, living in Arvada, Colorado with her husband and two teenage daughters. She squeezes writing romantic women's fiction into her already overloaded schedule. People watching at a *Campo di Fiori* sidewalk café inspired this short story.

Kathryn Mattingly lives in Portland, Oregon, where she enjoys teaching first grade at a small private school. Her story was inspired by love oozing out of the eternal city. Kathryn has just completed her second novel, and when not writing can be found spending time with her husband and four children.

Brian Moreland has written over twenty short stories and is currently working on his fourth novel. He also edited *Success Secrets of the Rich and Happy*, a non-fiction book for a motivational speaker. When not writing, Brian works as an international freelance video editor and Feng Shui consultant. He lives in Dallas, Texas. "The Portrait" was inspired on an outing to the market square at *Campo di Fiori*.

Larry Mulkerin is a cancer specialist and a clinical professor at the University of Washington. Larry wrote a textbook that was published by Medical Examination Publishing Company. He lectures and has done radio and television appearances, mostly related to Alternative Medicine issues. Still committed to medicine, Larry is also putting the wraps on his first novel, a thriller set in the Middle-East. "The Price of the Pope's Blessing" was inspired by attending a papal audience.

Myrna Murdoch lives in Honolulu with her daughter, Alexandra, who attends Punahou School. Myrna is a former stockbroker, retired from Morgan Stanley after a fifteen-year career.

Bill Neugent lives with his wife, Jill, in McLean, Virginia. He recently finished his first novel, a cyber-thriller. This piece is Bill's first experiment with the psycho-thriller genre. The piece was inspired by the MWC-Rome visit to the catacombs of Saint Callistus.

David Nutt, living quietly in Paris, writes for a cheese website he co-founded, Fromages.com. He is trying his hand at writing short stories to put a little bacon on the table. He recommends a Rome retreat for any aspiring writer; it puts the dots on the i. Thanks to the faculty for their time, hard work and encouragement.

John Oglesby lives in Memphis, Tennessee with his

world-traveling wife Jan, golf habit and writing addiction. He is an information technology manager with a major manufacturing firm and has published short stories and technical articles. He is currently at work on his next novel. This story was inspired by lovers at the Spanish Steps and the architectural design that uses the steps to link Bernini's fountain at the base with an obelisk and church at the top.

Mark E. Prose was born and raised in Wheat Ridge, Colorado. Mark graduated from Sts. Peter & Paul Elementary School, St. Regis Jesuit High School, the U.S. Merchant Marine Academy and Rensselaer Polytechnic Institute. The trip to Rome really was a pilgrimage.

Marie E. Reid was born in Philadelphia, is the mother of three and grandmother of eight. She has written two novels and is working on two more. She has one published poem, has attended the Maui Writers Conference every year since 1995, and the Maui Writers Retreat every year since 1997. When not writing, she works as an accountant, currently specializing in payroll. "Memories of a Lifetime" was written on the third anniversary of the death of her husband, James E. Reid.

Janette Ressue is a speech-language pathologist currently residing on the island of Maui. A novice creative writer, this is her first short story inspired by attending the Maui Writers Retreat in Rome. In addition to her continued pursuit of musical, artistic, travel and sports interests, she is now wrting her first novel.

Sandra Richardson is the last surviving member of a family of French/Celtic storytellers, lovers, liars and lunatics. A dual citizen, she lives in Taos, New Mexico and Sydney, Australia. This story was inspired by Rome street artists and a "what if" assignment: *What if your street portrait changes in your hotel room and magically appearing love* *tokens offer clues to re-finding your artist lover before leaving Rome?*

John Saul and Mike Sack have been working together for 25 years and have written more than two dozen New York Times Best Sellers which have been translated into 37 different languages. A number of their books have been in development for movies and television, and they have also authored plays and a best selling adventure computer game. Both Mr. Saul and Mr. Sack are active instructors and speakers at the Maui Writers Conference and Retreat.

Jack Smith lives in Castle Rock, Colorado with his yellow lab Buddy. He has completed Maui Fiction Retreat Tracks one, two, and three, and works managing a systems implementation project for a national company. Jack has completed a thriller about the Witness Protection Program, as well as a collection of short stories, and is currently at work on his second novel.

Mark Sylvester is an orthopedic surgeon and lives with his wife and son in Auburn, California. He began writing in 1995, to see if the right side of his brain still functioned. To date, he has finished an unpublished memoir and is working on his first novel.

Eldon Thompson, after washing out as a college quarterback, returned to his first love, writing. He may lack creativity, basic story sense, and the ability to spell, but he can recite, in order, all 26 letters of the English alphabet, and still throws a pretty mean spiral. He hopes to pick up the rest along the way. This piece was inspired by a visit to the site of Julius Caesar's assassination—home now to some 300 cats—and to the ruins of Pompeii. He also blames it on Daylight Savings, a lack of sleep, and his first ever glass of wine.

Coco Tralla lives in Denver, Colorado where she works full-time in the creative process of writing novels. Her two children, Alexa and Marcus, are the joy of her life as well as her two dogs, Oliver and Bella. In 2000, Coco won an Excellence in Writing Award at the Santa Barbara Writers Conference. After attending the Maui Writers retreat for the past two years, Coco continues to stay connected with her readers through her website at www.CocoTralla.com. "Hands of Dust" was inspired by Coco's first book about a vintner who adds a woman to his fermenting grapes to make the best, most sophisticated, wine in Napa Valley.

Leah Tribolo is a freelance writer currently residing in Frankfurt Germany. She has been living and working abroad in various countries for the last ten years. She shares her time and sanity with three cats, three children, a plethora of papers and one patient husband. Leah is currently working on her first novel.

John Tullius is the director of the Maui Writers Conference, the author of thirteen books, including co-author of the best seller *Body of a Crime* and *Against the Law*. He has written scores of articles for dozens of magazines including *Cosmopolitan, Playboy,* and *Town and Country,* and was a contributing editor for *Tennis Magazine.*

Suzanne Tyrpak lives in Colorado with her husband, David, two cats and a persistent raccoon. She has written an unpublished novel, and a non-fiction book, *Instant Intuition,* and has had numerous articles published in periodicals and newspapers. Suzanne placed first in Rocky Mountain Fiction Writers' 2001 Colorado Gold Writing Contest. Her contribution to this anthology was inspired by a church, an ancient gypsy woman, and a dozen blood-red roses left drowning in a fountain.

The Maui Writers Conference takes place during Labor Day weekend every year. For more information about the Conference, the Retreats, the Manuscript Marketplace, the Department of Continuing Education, or to order tapes from Conference presentations, contact:

The Maui Writers Conference
P.O. Box 1118
Kihei, Maui, Hawaii 96793
808-879-0061
www.mauiwriters.com